A HAMLYN POINTER BOOK

The
HUMAN
BODY

**The illustrations in this book have been
selected from the Hamlyn all-colour paperback
THE HUMAN BODY by Paul Lewis and David Rubenstein**

Published 1972 by
The Hamlyn Group Limited
London · New York · Sydney · Toronto
Hamlyn House, Feltham, Middlesex, England
© Copyright The Hamlyn Publishing Group Limited 1972
ISBN 0 600 34393 6
Printed by Officine Grafiche Arnoldo Mondadori,
Verona, Italy.

 A HAMLYN POINTER BOOK

The HUMAN BODY

By John Garratt
Illustrated by John Bavosi

HAMLYN
LONDON · NEW YORK · SYDNEY · TORONTO

Contents

SKIN AND TISSUE

The human body is covered with skin. The skin has two layers. The outer layer is called the *epidermis*. This is the part that peels off in blisters. The inner layer is the *dermis*.

The skin that you touch is the outer part of the epidermis and is made entirely of dead cells. These cells were alive once, but as they are pushed nearer and nearer the surface by new cells beneath them in the lower part of the epidermis, they become filled with a horny material called *keratin*. Each cell produces keratin within itself and by the time it reaches the skin surface it is a dead cell packed with keratin. The dead cell soon flakes off and is replaced by another cell.

Beneath the epidermis is the soft layer of skin called the dermis. In this are the blood vessels and nerves to the skin, and the sweat glands, coiled tubes that open on the surface as pores. The watery secretion from these glands helps to cool the body. There are more sweat glands on the forehead, the palms and the soles, than anywhere else on the body.

Hair is part of the skin, and grows from *hair follicles* in the dermis. Each hair is kept supple by a gland that supplies it with moisture. Attached to the hair is a tiny muscle that can pull the hair upright, "making your hair stand on end". Hairs are continually being shed and replaced. On average about 30 to 60 hairs fall out each day. Hair grows quickest in the beard, more slowly on the scalp, and slowest on the arms and legs.

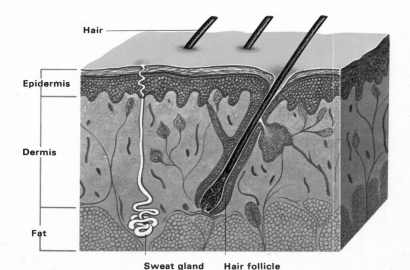

Right: This is a section of human skin showing the top layer, the epidermis, with the dermis under it, and beneath the dermis, the layers of fat which act as padding. A sweat gland and a hair follicle are also shown.

6

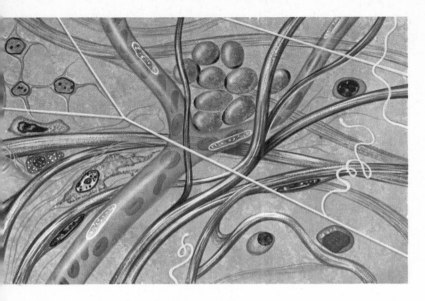

THE FUNCTIONS OF THE SKIN

The skin counts as an organ of the body and has certain jobs to do. It keeps out air and water and harmful germs. Because it is only loosely attached to the body, it causes blows to glance off. Nerve endings in the skin's deeper layer send back messages to the brain about what is felt.

The skin plays a big part in regulating the temperature of the body. If it is too hot, blood vessels in the skin grow wider and more blood is brought to the surface of the body which loses heat by radiation. At the same time the sweat glands pour out sweat which evaporates and thus cools the body. If the body is too cold, the blood vessels narrow, restricting the flow, so that less heat is lost.

The skin contains about one litre of blood circulating very slowly in the tiniest blood vessels. This blood is an emergency store for the body. The skin can also do some of the waste disposal job of the kidneys if these become inefficient.

A final protective job done by the skin is the keeping out of too much sunlight by producing a pigment which causes tanning of the skin.

CONNECTIVE TISSUE

The skin is supported by a framework of *connective tissue*. This has very few cells but a lot of tough fibrous and elastic tissue of various kinds. Blood vessels and nerves go through connective tissue and most of the fat in the body is stored in it.

THE SKELETON

The skeleton is the name given to the framework of bone and cartilage that supports and sometimes protects the softer parts of the body.

There are usually 206 bones in the human body. By the time a person is 25 years old, his skeleton has fully developed so that all the bone that began in cartilage is now bone. The skeleton does more than just support the body and protect vital parts. The bones are the body's calcium and phosphorus store, and the creator of red and many white blood cells (see p. 10).

THE BONES

Most of the bones in the human body are in the arms and legs. The four limbs together contain 126 bones.

The arm from shoulder to finger tips has 32 bones. These are: the *collar bone*, the *shoulder blade*, the bone of the upper arm (the *humerus*), the two bones of the forearm (the *radius* and the *ulna*), the 8 wrist bones, 5 bones in the palm (the *metacarpals*), 14 in the fingers (the *phalanges*). Each finger has 3 phalanges, and the thumb has two.

The leg has 31 bones. These are: the hip bone, the bone of the thigh (the *femur*, the biggest bone in the body), the kneecap (*patella*), the two bones of the lower leg (the *tibia* and *fibula*), 7 *tarsal* bones forming the heel and instep, 5 *metatarsals* between them and the 14 phalanges that form the toes. The big toe has two phalanges, the other toes, 3 each.

The remaining 80 bones in the human body are: the 8 *cranial* bones that surround the brain and protect it, the 14 bones of the face, the 3 bones in each ear, the *hyoid* bone in the throat, the 26 spine bones (7 in the neck, 12 in the chest, five in the small of the back plus the *sacrum* and the *coccyx*). The chest has 12 ribs on each side and one breastbone. (Some people have 13 pairs of ribs).

GROWTH AND HEIGHT

When the average boy is $17\frac{3}{4}$ and the average girl $16\frac{1}{4}$, they have reached their full height except for a slight lengthening of the spine over the next 12 years or so. In old age, a person becomes less tall than he or she was.

Opposite page: A front view of the human skeleton. All the bones in the body have Latin or Greek names and these are often used because sometimes no exact English name exists. For example, the name "Humerus" is used, not "the bone of the upper arm". A doctor is still likely to call a broken collar bone a fractured "clavicle".

The human skeleton is much the same as it was when man's ancestors were on four feet. It has adapted itself to the upright posture from the horizontal. The spine is not a straight upright rod of 26 bones, but appears curved when looked at from the side, in the shape of a letter S. The neck bones form a slight forward curve, the chest bones a backward curve, the *lumbar* bones a forward curve, the tail a backward curve. This is the natural curvature of the spine.

The skeletons seen in museums and anatomy classes have dried up. The "organic" matter (30 per cent) of the skeleton has decayed leaving the hard and brittle "inorganic" matter (70 per cent).

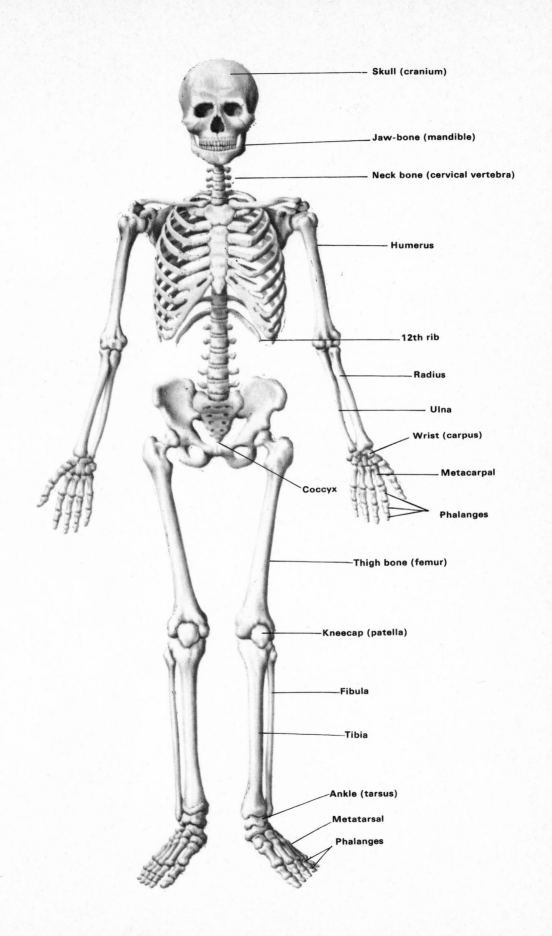

Skull (cranium)

Jaw-bone (mandible)

Neck bone (cervical vertebra)

Humerus

12th rib

Radius

Ulna

Wrist (carpus)

Metacarpal

Coccyx

Phalanges

Thigh bone (femur)

Kneecap (patella)

Fibula

Tibia

Ankle (tarsus)

Metatarsal

Phalanges

BONES AND JOINTS

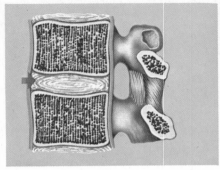

Cartilage is a softer material that holds many of the joints between bones together. When a baby is still in its mother's womb, all its bones are made of cartilage; and when a baby is born its bones are still soft. As the child grows up, the bones gradually harden as they grow.

Most bones have a compact outer layer and an inner network like a honeycomb, which is also very strong.

BONE MARROW

The inside of a bone is filled with *bone marrow*. Most marrow is yellow and made of fat cells, but in the first years of life all this marrow is red. It is full of blood-forming cells. Grown-ups have less red marrow. They have it only in the spine, the breast-bone, the ribs, pelvis and skull.

Above: A vertebral joint. These are the joints of the spine.

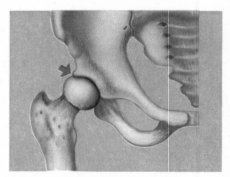

Above: A fibrous skull joint. The lines where the bones join are called sutures.

THE IMPORTANCE OF BONE

Bone is not only very strong – leg bones can resist pressure of a tonne or more – but it performs two important functions for the rest of the body. It stores the minerals essential for growth and health, and makes all the red blood cells and most of the white blood cells.

Calcium and phosphorus are the two most important minerals found in bone, but iron, magnesium, and fluorine are also found there. Because calcium and phosphorus are vital to so many of the chemical processes that keep the fluids of the body healthy, they are deposited, removed, and replaced according to need.

So the bones are not merely a strong framework. They are a crucial part of the body chemistry. If you look at the picture of the skeleton you will see that bones are of many different shapes. *Long* bones are generally shaped like a tube, but with thickened ends. *Short* bones are like those in the wrist and ankle. *Flat* bones are like those of the skull. *Irregular* bones are seen in the face and in the spine.

All these bones, with one exception, join other bones. Only the *hyoid* bone in the throat does not join another bone. (Hyoid means U-shaped.)

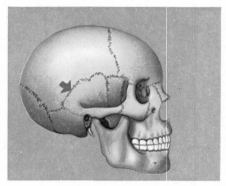

Above: A hinge joint. In this one the femur joins the tibia and fibula.

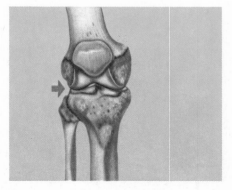

Above: A ball and socket joint. This one is where the femur joins the hip bone.

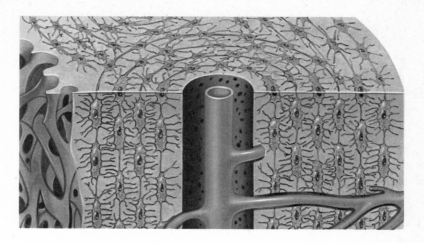

JOINTS AND CARTILAGE

When bone meets bone, there is a joint. A joint can be one where the bones, though joined, do not move; or one where plenty of movement occurs; or one where only a little movement can be made.

Cartilage (gristle) is a glassy-looking elastic tissue that helps to keep joints together. It also acts as a shock absorber at joints. For example, cartilage between each bone of the spine absorbs the shock, to the spine and brain, of landing heavily on your feet.

Cartilage acts as a centre of new bone manufacture while a child is growing up. It is found in adults as part of the bridge of the nose, in the ear flaps, in the throat and air passages, and the front part of the ribs.

LIGAMENTS

Ligaments are made of strong fibrous (stringy) tissue and their job is to hold movable joints together. It is possible to see how these ligaments work in a joint such as the knee. Violent movement of the wrong sort can "pull" a ligament.

So a joint that moves will not only have cartilage between the surfaces of the bones of the joint, but also ligaments to support it.

Above: This is a diagram of the hard outer part of a bone. The layers of bone are like the rings in a tree trunk. They contain bone cells and surround a central canal in which are blood vessels (shown here), nerves and lymph channels.

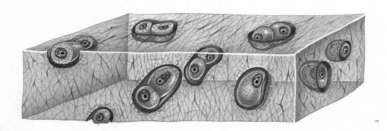

Left: This diagram shows the structure of cartilage as found in the ribs. The hard tissue contains oval or flattened cells.

11

MUSCLES AND MOVEMENT

Muscle tissue is like a bundle of fibres held together. These fibres are spindle-shaped. A typical muscle is thin at the ends and wider in the middle.

The muscles that can be moved at will are called voluntary or skeletal muscles. The involuntary muscles are not under conscious control.

Among the principle muscles are the *deltoid* (the muscle of the shoulder), the *pectorals* (the muscles on the front of the chest), the *biceps* and the *triceps* (in the arm), the *gastrocnemius* (the calf muscle) and the *gluteals* (in the buttocks).

VOLUNTARY MUSCLE

Voluntary muscles move the bones that make up the skeleton. There are about 656 muscles in the human body. The male body contains just over 40 per cent muscle in its total weight. The female body has about 6 per cent less.

Voluntary muscles are also called *striped* muscles since under a microscope their fibres show fine dark and light cross-markings. These fibres contract and relax to make the muscle move.

MUSCLE CONTRACTION

Most muscles are attached to bone at one end, occasionally both ends, by a *tendon*, which is made of the same kind of tissue as a ligament. All muscles have an *origin* and an *insertion*. The origin of a muscle is usually from a bone that the muscle does not move. The insertion is usually onto a bone that the muscle can move. The best-known muscle, the *biceps*, has its origin from the shoulder and is inserted into the main bone of the forearm in order to move the elbow joint.

When the fibres contract, a muscle becomes shorter and pulls on the bone it is inserted into. So the biceps contracts to bend the forearm, and its opposite muscle, the *triceps*, straightens the forearm when it contracts. Every muscle has an opposite number. The working of muscles across joints allows a very wide range of movements.

Below: The muscles of the human body seen from the front. The back also contains a complex arrangement of muscles.

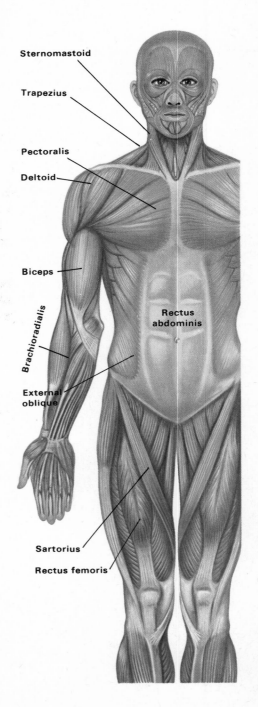

Sternomastoid
Trapezius
Pectoralis
Deltoid
Biceps
Brachioradialis
Rectus abdominis
External oblique
Sartorius
Rectus femoris

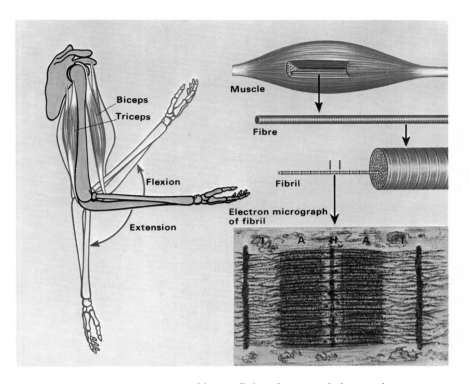

MUSCULAR ENERGY

When muscles shorten, energy is used up and heat is made. The fibres respond to nerve messages acting on protein in the muscle. The energy comes from glucose stored in the muscle. Like a car engine, some of this energy (about 25 per cent) is used to contract the muscle, while about 75 per cent is converted into heat. This is why muscular work makes you warm.

INVOLUNTARY MUSCLE

Involuntary muscle is muscle that cannot be moved at will. It is also called *smooth* muscle because it has no cross-markings on its individual cells, like voluntary muscle. It is found in the stomach, the intestines, the arteries, the veins and many other organs.

Unlike voluntary muscle, involuntary muscle contracts slowly and rhythmically (as in the movement of the intestine, which is called peristalsis) and is controlled by a part of the nervous system that is also not under conscious control.

Sometimes the voluntary muscles are not under voluntary control either. For example, when the body is cold and starts to shiver, the shivering is caused by the voluntary muscles contracting to to provide heat. They are stimulated to do this by involuntary nerve impulses.

Above: Pairs of antagonistic muscles alternately contract and relax to produce opposing movements. This diagram shows how the biceps bends the elbow joint and the triceps straightens it. It also shows that a muscle is made of fibres arranged in bundles. Each fibre is itself made of fibrils.

THE BRAIN AND THE NERVOUS SYSTEM

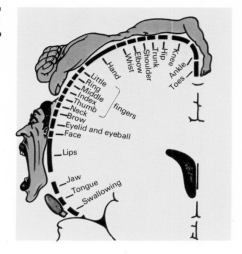

The brain weighs about 1·5 kg and almost fills the skull above the level of the bridge of the nose. It is soft, like a jelly, and nearly three-quarters of it consists of two large, heavily-grooved masses of nerve tissue, one on each side in the shape of a half sphere. They are known as the *cerebral hemispheres*. The remaining quarter of the brain, looked at from above, is hidden by these two lumps.

The remaining quarter contains the *mid-brain*, the *cerebellum* (or little brain) and the *medulla*, which is at the meeting of the brain and the beginning of the spinal cord.

THE CEREBRAL HEMISPHERES

The cerebral hemispheres are in charge of all conscious activity. Thinking, remembering, understanding – all such things depend on them. This is why they are bigger in man than in any other animal. In particular, the outer layer of grey matter, called the *cortex*, is the basis of mind. It covers the surface of the hemispheres and is crumpled and wrinkled. This is the newest part of man's brain and is the seat of the intellect, as opposed to the lower "old" parts of the brain where the automatic activity of the body is controlled.

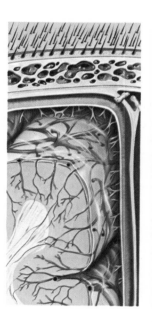

Above top: This diagram shows how parts of the body are represented in the brain cortex.

Above: A section through the skull showing the various layers that protect the brain. There is also a protective layer of fluid in the membranes between the skull and brain.

Left: The left cerebral hemisphere. The red area is where movement is controlled, the green where sensations are analyzed, the yellow where speech is controlled, the orange where hearing, and the blue where vision, are analyzed.

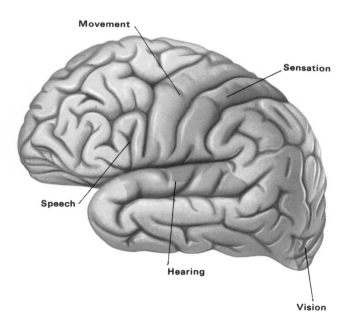

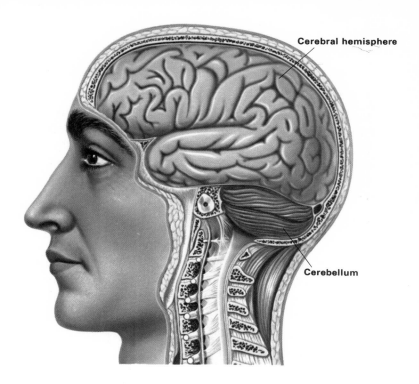

Right: This diagram of the side of the neck and head shows the brain lying in the skull. The convoluted part is the left cerebral hemisphere, with the cerebellum immediately below it at the back.

Cerebral hemisphere

Cerebellum

THE CEREBRAL CORTEX

Under the cortex is a mass of white tissue that conveys messages to and from the grey matter. The cortex itself forms four lobes on each side which perform different functions.

The *frontal* lobes are situated above the eyes and behind the forehead. They are concerned with personality, behaviour and movement, including speech. Further back are the *parietal* lobes whose

Right: A sketch of the lobes of the brain. The *frontal* lobe is shown green, the *parietal* lobe yellow, the *temporal* lobe orange, and the *occipital* lobe red.

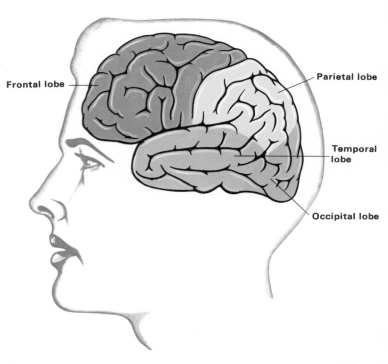

Frontal lobe

Parietal lobe

Temporal lobe

Occipital lobe

job is to analyze sensations and how the body exists in relation to its surroundings.

The parietal lobes have fine discrimination. They distinguish between degrees of heat and cold and detect detailed differences of shape, texture and size, for example. The more basic, or "crude" sensations, such as simply "hot" or "cold", are detected lower in the brain.

The *occipital* lobes are at the back of the brain. They are the brain's headquarters for eyesight.

On either side of the brain lies a separate projection, called the temporal lobe. The *temporal* lobe is the brain centre for interpreting hearing (it is part of the brain nearest the ear). This lobe, too, is probably associated with memory.

The brain is covered with three layers of tissue and inside the brain are four cavities, joined together, through which a special fluid circulates, as a shock absorber for the brain tissue. Around these cavities is more grey matter – grey, like the cortex, because it is full of nerve cells. The white matter all around it is made of nerve fibres.

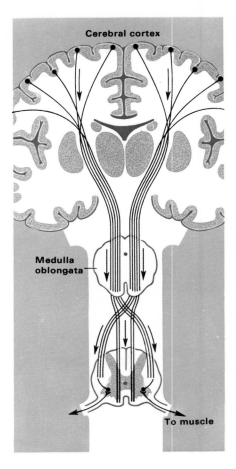

Above: This shows how messages from the cortex pass down through the brain in tracts of white matter (the long thin black lines in the diagram).

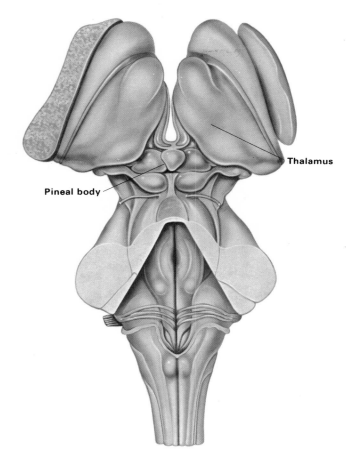

Left: A view of the brain beneath the cerebral hemispheres which shows the position of the *thalamus*, a nerve centre that transmits sensory feelings to the higher part of the brain (the cortex). The *pineal body* is a small gland that has no known function in the human body and is probably a remnant of the "third eye" of reptiles.

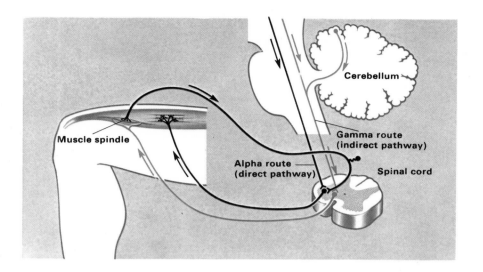

THE MID-BRAIN AND THE CEREBELLUM

Below the hemispheres is the *mid-brain*. It contains a number of cells that control movements of the body and others that are the centres of sleep and wakefulness. Beneath this is the *bridge*, a part of the brain connected with the two halves of the cerebellum and lying between the midbrain and the *medulla*.

The main job of the *cerebellum*, which has two lobes and lies under the back of the cerebral hemispheres, is to control muscle movement. It also helps the body to maintain balance, because of its close links with the balance organs of the ear.

Above This shows how muscle movements are controlled from the cerebellum by what is called the gamma route.

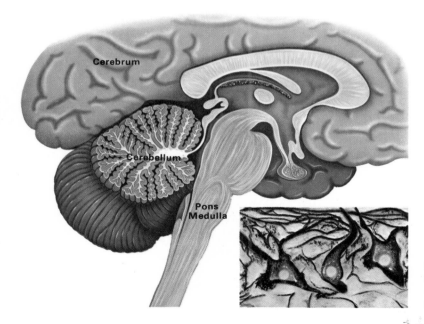

Left: A side view of the right side of the brain to show the position of the cerebellum. The smaller picture (*inset*) shows the special cells of the cerebellum.

17

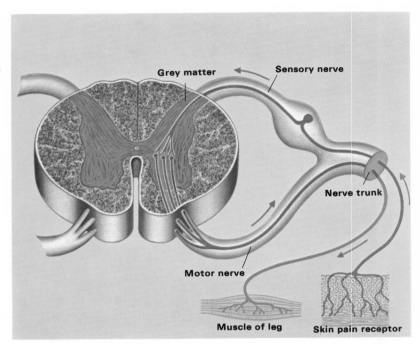

Grey matter

Sensory nerve

Nerve trunk

Motor nerve

Muscle of leg

Skin pain receptor

THE MEDULLA AND THE SPINAL CORD

The *medulla* is about two and a half cm long and looks like a thickening at the beginning of the spinal cord. It regulates vital functions such as breathing, blood pressure, and the heart beat.

The *spinal cord* runs inside the spinal column – a distance of 46 cm – from the bottom of the skull to the small of the back, and then becomes a pony tail of nerve tissue. The cord is about one cm wide.

THE NERVES

The brain is the site of twelve pairs of nerves to look after the special senses of seeing, hearing, taste and smell.

The spinal cord provides 31 pairs of nerves for the trunk and limbs.

A butterfly-shaped core of grey nerve cells forms a column from neck to tail in the centre of the cord, with white nerve fibres around it. The cells at the front are the ones for making the muscles move. Cells at the back look after feeling. The white fibres carry information about movement and sensation to and from the brain.

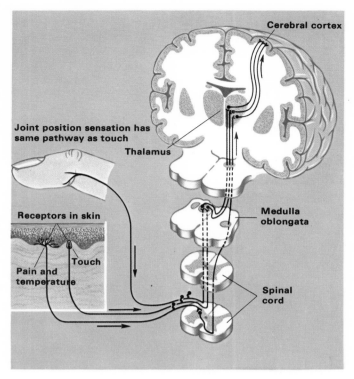

Joint position sensation has same pathway as touch

Thalamus

Receptors in skin

Touch

Pain and temperature

Medulla oblongata

Spinal cord

Left: Sensations of pain, temperature, touch, and of the position of joints pass up the spinal cord to the brain. All the information they send is in the form of nerve impulses.

A spinal nerve has a *motor* branch from the front, and a *sensory* branch from the back of the spinal cord, joined together. Branches of these nerves run to all the body organs giving off smaller and smaller branches.

The illustrations show how *reflexes* work and also explain the *sensation* in nerve endings.

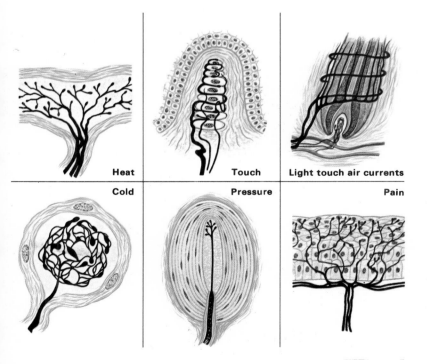

Heat

Touch

Light touch air currents

Cold

Pressure

Pain

Left: the chief means of feeling are nerve endings in the skin. The nerve endings for different senses are of different shapes. There are more pain endings than any other. Next in number come touch endings, then heat, and then cold. The human body detects cold and warmth far less precisely than other feelings.

THE EYE AND VISION

The eye is the organ of sight. It is shaped like a ball but is not a perfect sphere. It is about two and a half cm across in an adult and weighs seven gm.

Each eyeball is covered with a thick white covering. This covering has a clear section, called the *cornea*, over the front of the eye where light waves enter. Behind it is a space filled with a clear fluid. Behind the space is the *iris*, the coloured part of the eye. The opening in the iris is the *pupil*. Around the pupil is a ring of muscle that contracts in bright light to narrow the pupil. In dim light it relaxes to widen the pupil. Fear and other emotions can alter the size of the pupil.

THE LENS

Light coming through the pupil passes through the *lens*, a soft yellowish sphere with muscles attached to its rim. These muscles can alter the shape of the lens depending upon whether the object being looked at is near or distant. The lens has no blood in it and is nourished by the liquid on either side of it. Behind the lens is the *vitreous humour*, a sticky jelly which fills up the greater part of the cavity of the eye, and behind this is the *retina*.

THE RETINA AND COLOUR VISION

The *retina* is like a photographic film and has several layers of nerve cells. They convert light into nerve

Below: The parts of the eye. The *sclera* is the outer covering of the eye. It is continuous with the *cornea* which is transparent. The *vitreous humour* is the jelly-like fluid that fills the cavity of the eye behind the *lens*.

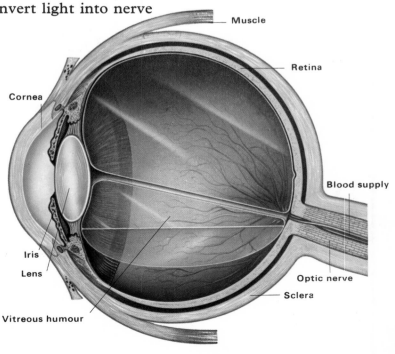

Muscle

Retina

Cornea

Blood supply

Iris

Lens

Optic nerve

Sclera

Vitreous humour

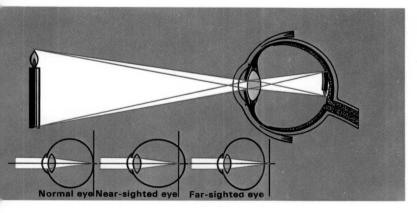

Normal eye   Near-sighted eye   Far-sighted eye

Left: When the eye looks at an object
— a candle in this picture — the retina
receives the image upside down and
smaller than the actual object. In
short sight the image is focused in
front of the retina, while in long sight
the image is focused behind the retina.

impulses which go to the brain by the optic nerve,
which connects the back of the eye to the brain.

Light waves arriving on the retina have been
focused partly by the lens and partly by the cornea.
The "picture" on the retina is upside down, and
much smaller than the original. In the brain, however, these nerve impulses are interpreted correctly
so that we see things as they are and not upside down
or minute.

The light-sensitive cells of the *retina* are called
rods and *cones*. Rods are for night vision and only
recognize shades of grey. Cones are for day vision
and can detect colours. There are more rods away
from the centre of the retina than at its centre. So
this part of the retina is best for seeing at night. The
"blind spot" is the part of the retina where the optic
nerve leaves the eye and at this point there are no rods
or cones.

STEREOSCOPIC SIGHT

The human eyes also have *stereoscopic vision*. This
means that you see better with two eyes than with one
because objects are seen in perspective. It is possible
to judge how near or far away objects are, and how
big they are in relation to one another.

DEFECTIVE EYESIGHT

Spectacles are said to have been invented by an
Italian monk in 1299. Today, people whose eyes do
not focus properly can see as clearly as those with
normal sight, when they have their glasses on.

Short-sighted people have too long an eye or too
powerful a lens, so that the light waves coming into
the eye come to a focus in front of the retina instead
of on it.

Below: This diagram shows that
objects on the right or left are seen by
both eyes, but that the optic nerve
fibres partly cross over so that all
objects on the left are "seen" by the
right side of the brain while those on
the right are "seen" by the left side.

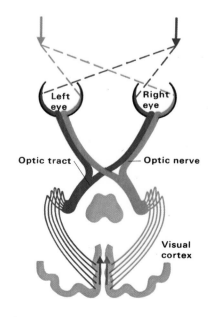

Left eye   Right eye

Optic tract   Optic nerve

Visual
cortex

Long-sighted people have too short an eye or too weak a lens, so that the light waves come to a focus behind the retina.

Astigmatic people have an abnormal cornea and the horizontal light waves are out of focus with the vertical rays.

Some people have *night-blindness*, and they cannot see as well as they should when the light is dim. A normal eye can increase its sensitivity to light about 75,000 times when in darkness. In *day-blindness* the eye can see normally when the light is not very strong, but cannot see so well when it is bright.

COLOUR BLINDNESS

These errors are not common but *colour blindness* is. About 8 per cent of white people in Europe and America are colour blind and colour blindness is much commoner in men than in women. But all of us are colour blind in bad light and red is the first colour to become indistinguishable as dusk approaches. In the morning, blue is the colour first visible.

Retinal cones, sensitive to red, blue, or green, the three primary colours, enable the human eye to see colour. All colours are derived from these three.

The commonest type of colour blindness is when red, yellow and green are confused. It is also fairly common to confuse yellow and orange, or red, yellow and green. One advantage of being colour blind is that it is easier to detect camouflage.

EYELIDS, EYEBROWS AND TEARS

It is not only the eyeball and brain that are concerned with sight. Eyebrows may keep sweat from the eyes, but the eyelids and eyelashes protect the eye. The eyelid is closed by a ring of muscles surrounding the eye and the upper lid has a special muscle to raise it.

In the upper and outer part of each eye is the tear gland that produces tears all the time. Tears go over the eye's surface to keep it clean and moist, and into the inner side of the eye. There, a little channel takes tears into the nose. Humans are the only animals that cry when upset, but anything that irritates the eye can cause a lot of tears. What cannot be carried away to the nose flows onto the cheeks. With a cold, the channel may be blocked, which is why people with bad colds or hay fever have watery eyes.

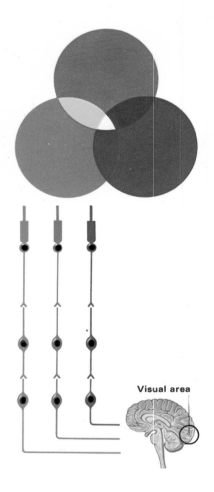

Above: Colour vision depends upon the mixing of the messages from three types of cone cell corresponding to the three primary colours. The brain interprets the message. All colours are a mixture of the three primary colours. The retina contains three types of cone cell to detect the three primary colours. When an image falls on the retina, the cone cells transmit information to the brain about the relative amounts of each primary colour the image contains. The brain interprets the message and registers the single colour that can be made from the mixture.

THE EAR, HEARING AND BALANCE

The ear is the organ of hearing. There is an outer, a middle and an inner ear. The outer ear consists of the flap of the ear and the passage that leads down to the eardrum. Sounds are funnelled into this passage but the ear flap in humans plays very little part in catching sounds. In many animals this part of the ear is more important. When sounds reach the eardrum or *tympanic membrane* they make it vibrate.

THE EARDRUM

The eardrum lies at the end of the six cm of passage from the ear flap. It separates the outer and middle ears. When it vibrates the vibrations are transmitted to the three bones of the middle ear: the *hammer*, which touches the inner surface of the drum, the *anvil*, and the *stirrup*. These tiny bones join together, and the stirrup touches the inner ear. This part of the inner ear is called the *cochlea* (it is shaped like a snail and cochlea is Latin for snail). An oval window in the cochlea, only $\frac{1}{16}$th of the area of the ear drum, receives the vibrations. The cochlea is a coiled tube in the bone of the skull. It contains the actual organ of hearing – special nerve processes resting on a layer of fibres.

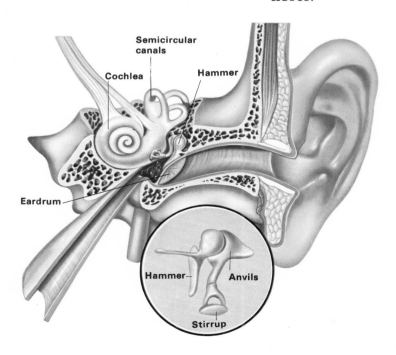

Left: A diagram of the human ear. The ear drum separates the outer ear from the middle ear. The circular picture (*inset*) shows the three little bones in the middle ear, the hammer, the anvil and the stirrup. They transmit the vibrations of the drum to the inner ear which contains the organ of hearing.

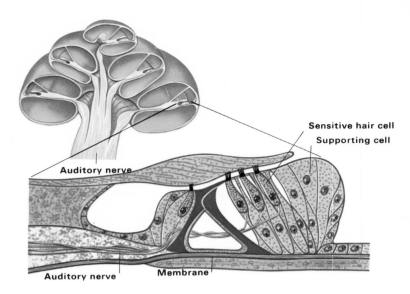

Sensitive hair cell
Supporting cell

Auditory nerve

Auditory nerve

Membrane

HEARING

Sound vibrations cause tiny pressure changes in the cochlear fluid, and the minute pressure waves, act on the special nerve processes which send messages through the hearing nerve to the brain. These waves reflect the loudness of a sound and its pitch. When these impulses reach the brain they are interpreted as sound. The organ of hearing has different areas to deal with high and low sounds, just as a piano keyboard does.

THE EUSTACHIAN TUBE

Leading from the hollow of the middle ear down to the back of the throat is a tube called the *Eustachian* tube (named after the anatomist Eustachius). This tube keeps the pressure in the middle ear the same as the outside air pressure. It is this pressure that alters when you fly, causing a temporary deafness. A bad cold can block this tube, which is why people are advised not to fly when they have a cold.

VOLUME AND DIRECTION OF SOUND

Intensity of noise is measured in *decibels*. A whisper is reckoned to be 30 decibels, conversation 60 decibels.

Human ears do not have as good a sense of where sound is coming from as have the ears of some other animals, but two ears are better at this job than one alone, and can tell the direction of sound to within 3 degrees.

Above: A diagram showing the fluid-filled tube that coils round inside the cochlea (*top left*). The central part of this coil is shown enlarged (*bottom*). The corresponding parts are keyed by black lines. This central part is where sounds are finally received before going to the brain through the nerve of hearing, the *auditory nerve.*

Right: This shows how messages reach the brain from the parts of the ear concerned with balance. The *labyrinth* is the name given to these organs of balance and the vestibular nerve runs from them on each side of the head to the cortex, the cerebellum, and the spinal cord.

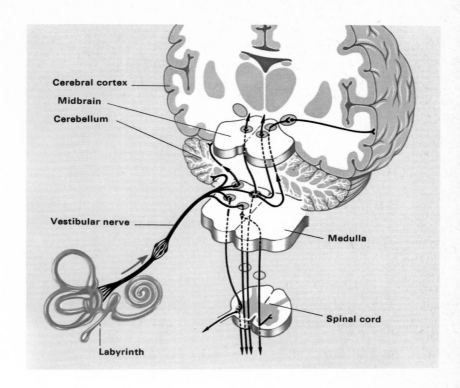

Cerebral cortex
Midbrain
Cerebellum
Vestibular nerve
Medulla
Spinal cord
Labyrinth

DEAFNESS

There are two main types of deafness. In one, the sounds do not reach the inner ear. This can be caused by an excess of wax in the ear. In the other, the sounds reach the inner ear but are not transmitted to the brain properly.

BALANCE

The ear also contains other parts, deep in the skull, that are concerned with balance. Together, these parts are the *labyrinth*. One part is formed by two containers with hairs and chalky particles inside. With it, a person knows, without conscious effort, which way up he is in relation to the earth – the sense of gravity.

The other part is made of three canals filled with fluid and called the *semicircular canals*. Each contains a bundle of sensitive nerves. When the head is moved around, the fluid in the canals moves and stimulates the nerves. They send nerve impulses to the brain. The three canals are at right angles to each other so that movement in any direction can be detected; up, down or sideways. This information goes to the grey matter of the brain cortex, to the cerebellum, and to the spinal cord.

Below: This is a model of the three semicircular canals, the main parts of the organs of balance. There is one for each direction, up, down and sideways. Their job is to detect and respond to rotation of the head in any direction.

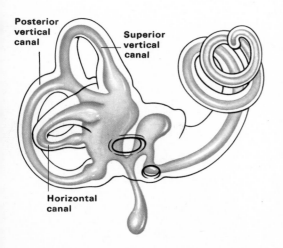

Posterior vertical canal
Superior vertical canal
Horizontal canal

25

TASTE
AND SMELL

THE TONGUE

The human tongue has about 3000 taste buds with which to distinguish one taste from another. Four basic tastes – sweet, sour, salt and bitter – are detected by different parts of the tongue. There are also taste buds on the tonsils, the roof of the mouth and further back in the throat.

TASTE BUDS

The taste bud itself is like a nest of long cells connected to a sensitive nerve that takes messages to the brain. In spite of being used to detect four different basic tastes, all taste buds look alike. On the tongue the taste buds are mainly on the tip, the back and the sides. The centre of the tongue is not used to taste with.

Sweetness and saltiness are tasted mainly at the tip of the tongue, sourness at the sides, bitterness at the back.

THE SENSE OF SMELL

Taste is sometimes confused with smell. It is easy to mistake a smell for a taste. An onion, for instance, has no taste. Anyone with a heavy cold or other nose congestion may complain that he has lost his sense of taste. In fact, what he has lost is his sense of smell.

Below right: A taste bud. It consists of a number of long cells connected to a sensory nerve.

Below left: This shows the position of different taste buds on the tongue. At the tip, they detect sweet and salt things. At the sides they detect sour tastes. At the back, they detect bitter tastes. The centre of the surface of the tongue can hardly taste anything.

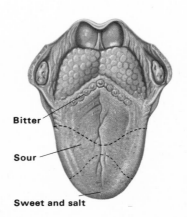

Bitter

Sour

Sweet and salt

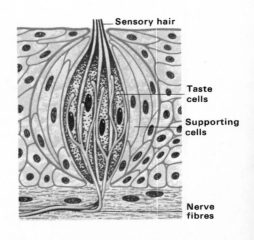

Sensory hair

Taste cells

Supporting cells

Nerve fibres

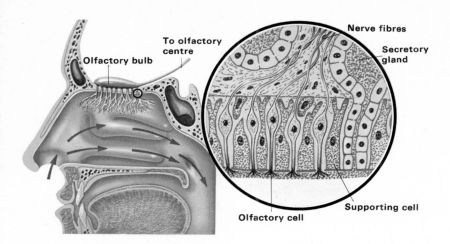

Olfactory bulb

To olfactory centre

Nerve fibres

Secretory gland

Olfactory cell

Supporting cell

Above: A side view of the nose. It shows the nerves for smelling, which have their endings in the uppermost part of the cavity of the nose. These *olfactory nerve* cells are shown in the circular picture (*inset*). At the lower end of each cell are long hair-like lashes. They detect the smells that are breathed in. The olfactory bulb collects these nerve impulses and transmits them to the olfactory centre in the brain.

In the human body the sense of taste is not as finely developed as the sense of smell. The nose is a much better detective than the tongue.

THE NOSE

Smell is detected by the nose. The cells that deal with smells are on the upper and inner surfaces of the nose. They are cells with long hairs on them that are covered with a layer of liquid *mucus*. Smells have to be dissolved in this before a cell can detect them.

From these cells runs, on each side of the nose, the *olfactory nerves*. These pass through small openings in the bone of the skull to join the *olfactory bulb*, where there are more nerve cells to transmit messages to the brain. The bulb is just beneath the front lobe of the brain.

Although it is said that man can detect more than 10,000 different smells, his sense of smell is much less fine than a dog's. This is because man has developed in such a way that smell is less important in his everyday life, and his brain has less room for dealing with smell. That part is devoted to "higher things".

A person's sense of smell dulls very quickly. If he is in a room containing a particular smell, he soon ceases to notice it.

The sense of smell becomes less sensitive in old age. There is a danger that old people may be poisoned by gas because they cannot detect a gas leak.

Injury to the nose or the olfactory nerves in the skull can also cause loss of the sense of smell, whilst blockage of the nasal passages due to a cold can also affect it temporarily.

THE VOICE AND SPEECH

Speech is the way in which humans express, in sound, their feelings and thoughts. Speech can be divided into three parts – the sounds, the shaping of them (just making a sound is not speech), and the control of them.

THE LARYNX AND VOCAL CORDS

Sounds are produced in the voice box, or *larynx*, in the throat. Air from the lungs makes the *vocal cords* vibrate. Small muscles in the larynx alter the tension on the cords, which alters the pitch of the sounds.

CONTROLLING SOUND

Shaping the sounds, *articulation*, is done by the muscles of the jaws, lips, tongue, and the roof of the mouth. They alter the shape of the hollow spaces in the mouth and throat, and can interrupt a stream of sound.

The control of these sounds depends on the speech centre of the brain. In most people this centre is in the left side of the brain but in a few (who are also left-handed), it is in the right side. If this area is injured or diseased, speech will be affected.

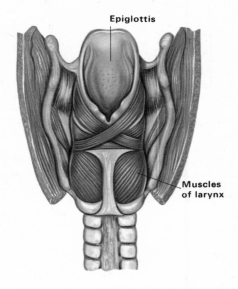

Above: A back view of the *larynx*. The muscles control the vocal cords. The *epiglottis* is a leaf-like piece of cartilage that prevents food "going down the wrong way" past the larynx into the lungs.

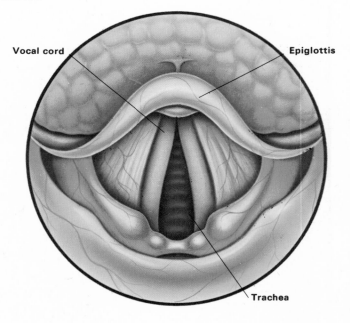

Right: A view of the larynx from above. The wedge-shaped opening is just over one cm long in men (less in women) and is bordered by the vocal cords. If the cords (which are membranes) are brought together, and air blows from the lungs, a sound is formed. Vibrations of the vocal cords occur many times a second.

KEEPING WARM

Man is a warm-blooded animal but not as warm as a dog, cat, horse, cow, pig, sheep or chicken. The normal temperature of 98·4°F (37°C) is no more than an average, since body temperature is lower in the morning and higher in the evening. Very young children are warmer, and old people colder, than normal.

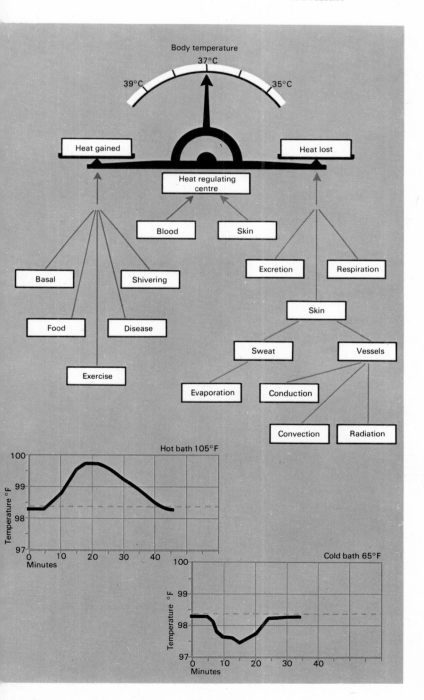

Left: This diagram shows how the body's temperature is controlled by balancing heat gained against heat lost. The heat regulating centre is in a part of the brain called the *hypothalamus*. It contains nerve cells that are sensitive to any heat changes in the blood supplied to them.

A fall in blood temperature sets off automatic nerve impulses that narrow the skin's blood vessels to keep in heat, and makes the muscles "shiver" to generate more heat.

A rise in blood temperature provokes heat loss by widening the blood vessels and by sweating.

The diagram also shows the main ways in which heat is made in the body and lost.

Health depends on the body being at the right temperature. This is 37°C (98·4°F on most thermometers used at home).

In the diagram the word "basal" refers to the everyday energy, that is heat produced by the cells at work. Muscular work increases this basal level.

29

THE HEART AND CIRCULATION

The human heart is a hollow lump of muscle lying in the chest between the lungs. About one third of it lies to the right of the breastbone, and two thirds to the left. The apex (tip) of the heart normally lies between the fifth and sixth ribs, nine cm to the left of the breastbone.

The purpose of the heart is to pump the blood round the body. Every minute, all the blood in the body passes once through the heart. The heart is really two pumps. One sends blood through the lungs, and the other through the rest of the body.

The heart beats about 70 times a minute and each beat pumps about 60 gm of blood. Exercise, worry, and excitement are some of the things that make it beat faster.

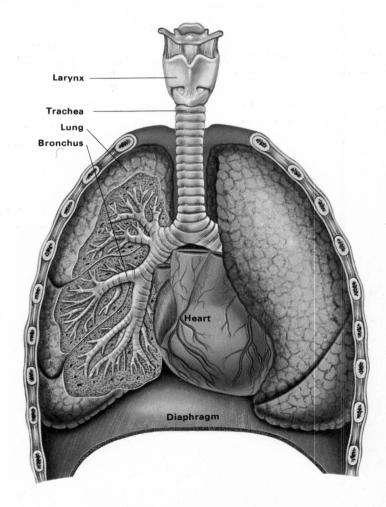

Larynx

Trachea

Lung

Bronchus

Heart

Diaphragm

Right: The chest with front cut away, showing the position of the heart and lungs. The cavity of the chest is enclosed at the bottom by the diaphragm and above by the bottom of the neck and the upper ribs. The 12 spine bones behind (not visible here) and the curved ribs and breastbone in front, all protect the chest.

30

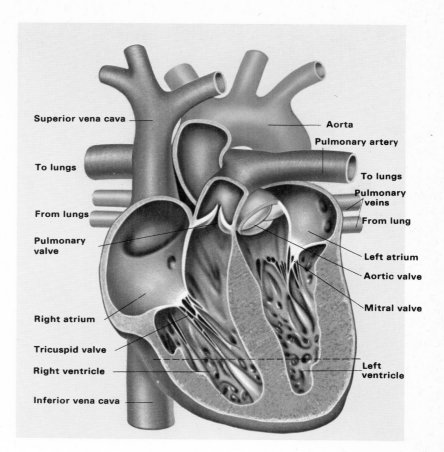

Labels on the figure:
Superior vena cava — Aorta
Pulmonary artery
To lungs — To lungs
Pulmonary veins
From lungs — From lung
Pulmonary valve — Left atrium
Aortic valve
Mitral valve
Right atrium
Tricuspid valve
Right ventricle — Left ventricle
Inferior vena cava

Right: This is a model of the heart and the main blood vessels going to and from it. The biggest blue tube represents the *venae cavae*, the big veins that return blood to the heart from the upper and lower parts of the body. The *pulmonary artery*, unlike other arteries, carries unoxygenated blood. It delivers venous (blue) blood to the lungs where oxygen will make it red, before it returns by the pulmonary veins (which carry oxygenated blood).

CIRCULATION OF THE BLOOD

The heart has four hollow spaces, called chambers. The upper two are the *atria*; the lower larger two, the *ventricles* (ventricle means a little stomach). The ventricles pump blood into the lungs and the rest of the body, and the atria collect blood from the veins.

The blood leaves the heart and goes through the *arteries* to the body organs and tissues. It is coloured bright red. It then goes through very small blood vessels called *capillaries* before returning to the heart through the *veins*. This venous blood is a bluish colour because it has lost its oxygen.

Venous blood enters the right atrium, which then pumps it into the right ventricle. This ventricle pumps it round the lungs, and it then enters the left atrium. The left atrium pumps it into the left ventricle, the biggest and strongest chamber, which pumps it round the body.

The cardiac cycle is the routine activity of the heart during a single heart beat. In each cycle, the

Right: These diagrams show the first part of a series of events during a single heart beat. In (a) the atria fill with blood. Pressure of blood opens the valves to the ventricles and they fill with blood. The cycle begins with contractions of the atria (b) which force more blood into the ventricles.

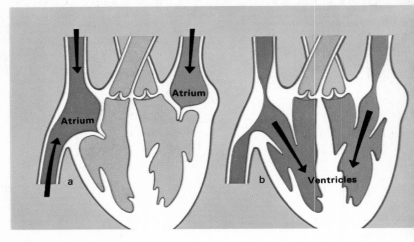

two atria contract simultaneously, forcing blood into the ventricles. Then the ventricles contract pushing the blood to the lungs and body. The walls of the ventricles are much thicker than the walls of the atria because they have heavier work to do.

THE HEARTBEAT

Between the atria and ventricles, and between the ventricles and the two big blood vessels leading from them (the aorta and the pulmonary artery), are one-way valves. The aorta is the big artery that leads into the system of arteries that carry the blood throughout the body. If you listen to a heartbeat it makes a sound usually described "lub-dub". The first sound is that of the ventricles contracting and the shutting of the valves between them and the atria. The second sound is the shutting of the *semilunar* valves to the big blood vessels.

The valves between the atria and ventricles, are the *mitral valve*, on the left, and the *tricuspid valve*,

Below left: A diagram of the blood supply of the heart itself. These arteries are the coronary arteries. Disease causing narrowing or blockage of these arteries is the cause of "coronaries".

Below: A cross-section of the heart cut across the ventricles. It shows how much thicker the muscle wall of the left ventricle is than that of the right. The left ventricle is the more powerful pump.

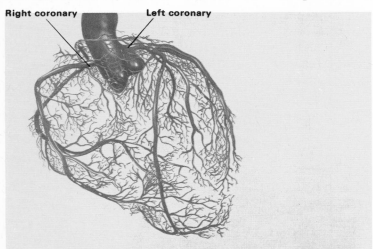

Right coronary   Left coronary

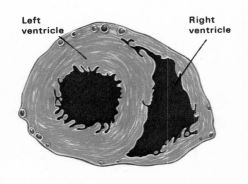

Left ventricle   Right ventricle

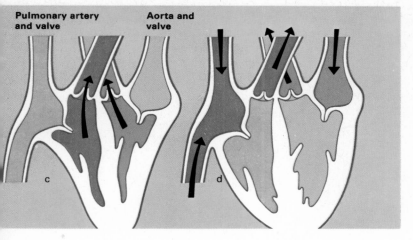

Pulmonary artery and valve   Aorta and valve

c   d

Left: (The continuation of the cardiac cycle). In (c) the ventricles contract. Pressure in them is greater than in the atria so the valves between them snap shut. While these valves are closing, the ventricular pressure is more than the pressure in the aorta and pulmonary artery, so blood flows into them. Then the ventricles relax, pressure falls, these valves close and the cycle begins again (d).

on the right. The mitral valve has two flaps (like a bishop's mitre), the other, three. When shut, they prevent blood flowing back into the atria.

The other valves are the *aortic valve*, between the aorta and the left ventricle, and the *pulmonary valve*, between the right ventricle and the pulmonary artery to the lungs. Because they are shaped like half-moons, they are also called *semilunar* valves. If any of these valves ceases to work properly, surgeons can sometimes replace it with an artificial valve.

THE PULSE

The *pulse* is the heartbeat felt in the arteries. This can sometimes be seen in a person's neck or at the other places where an artery is near the body surface.

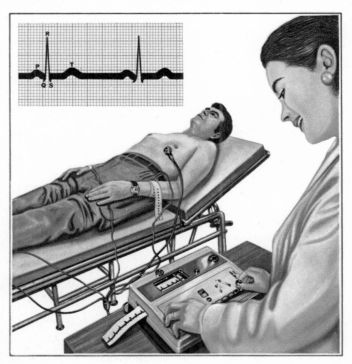

Left: The man lying on the table is having the electrical activity of his heart recorded on a machine called an electrocardiogram. Electrical activity of each part of the heart has its own wave form. The record (*inset*) shows how the wave is studied. P comes from the contracting atria, QRS from the contracting ventricles, and T coincides with relaxation of the ventricles.

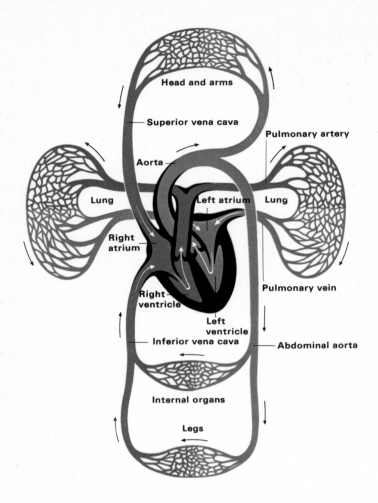

Left: A diagram of the circulation of the blood. The blood goes round and round inside this network. At the junction between the arteries and veins are tiny thin-walled vessels called capillaries which supply food and oxygen to the cells. They are linked with the veins by tiny venules and carry waste matter from the cells to the veins. In this way the blood returns through the veins to the heart.

The pulse is usually taken at the wrist, and its rapidity and strength of beat help doctors to make a diagnosis (identify a disease).

BLOOD PRESSURE

Blood pressure is the pressure of blood in the arteries. It is a guide to the tension in the muscular elastic walls of the arteries, big and small. The tension is produced by the pumping of the blood through these tubes by the heart. As the heart beats it meets with a certain amount of resistance from the narrow tubes it is beating against.

The pressure depends on two things: the output of blood by the heart, and the resistance of blood vessels, especially the medium-sized and smaller arteries.

A doctor measures this blood pressure with a machine called a *sphygmomanometer*. He puts a stocking-like bag around the arm and blows it up with a little pump. At the same time as he is letting

Below: This cross-section shows that the wall of an artery is thicker than that of a vein.

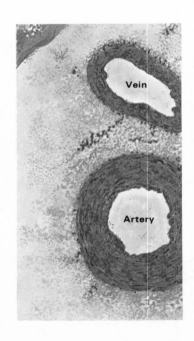

the air out again he listens to the big artery in front of the elbow. The appearance and disappearance of the sounds he hears, mark the pressure of the blood when the heart is pushing the blood out, and the pressure when the heart is about to fill again. He measures this by a column of mercury joined to the bag. When he hears the sounds he is listening for, he notes the mercury level at the time. Blood pressure is expressed in mm of mercury. The average blood pressure in a young adult is 120 mm mercury for the first sound, and 80 mm for the second.

The muscles in the artery walls can narrow the artery or widen it. This activity is influenced by one of the vital centres of the brain. Nervous messages go to this centre all the time, from special nerve endings, especially in the walls of the *aorta* (the big artery leading from the heart). So the centre continuously supervises and adjusts the blood pressure to keep it steady. If the pressure is too high, the centre lowers it by relaxing the arteries, and vice versa.

HIGH BLOOD PRESSURE

High blood pressure is not necessarily abnormal. If you get excited, annoyed or worried, the heart quickens and the arteries narrow. An angry man can raise his blood pressure quite considerably. The anxiety of a visit to the doctor is often enough to raise the blood pressure temporarily.

High blood pressure can be a disease, or a sign of disease. A damaged kidney, for example, can cause it. So can too much of the hormone *noradrenaline* from the adrenal glands.

Prolonged high blood pressure makes the walls of the arteries thicken. This, in turn reduces the width of them, cutting down the flow of blood. The

Below right: These drawings show the various thicknesses of the walls of blood vessels and the varying width of the tube which carries the blood. An *arteriole* is a small artery. A capillary is made of one thickness of cell and is no wider than one red blood corpuscle.

Below: This shows the meeting of the red blood (arterial) side of the circulation and the blue (venous) side. In between are the capillaries.

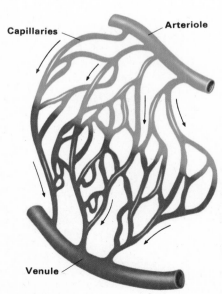

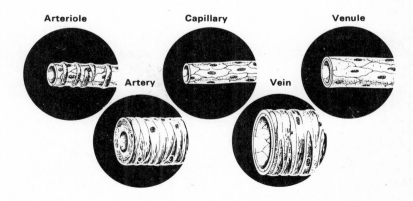

decreased blood supply can damage the kidney, heart or brain. The arteries also gradually harden with age, though this need not necessarily lead to a particularly high blood pressure.

SHOCK

Shock is a state the body gets into, often following severe injury and loss of blood. The patient's blood pressure is low, the pulse rapid, while sweating, cold hands and feet and loss of consciousness are the other signs.

All these can be understood as the body's habit, when blood is lost, to send what remains to the organs that are vital – the brain and the kidneys – so that they get enough oxygen and glucose.

When blood is lost and the patient is shocked the small blood vessels in the skin and muscles narrow in order to keep up the blood pressure. Narrowed blood vessels in the skin make the patient cold and white.

Below: This diagram shows the reaction of the body to rapid bleeding. When the level falls as low as shown (2) the body shunts blood to vital organs such as the brain and kidneys. The hormones from the adrenal gland help by making the heart beat faster to push out blood. They also cause the blood vessels to narrow to maintain normal blood pressure. The pressure rises because the heart is now pumping through narrower tubes.

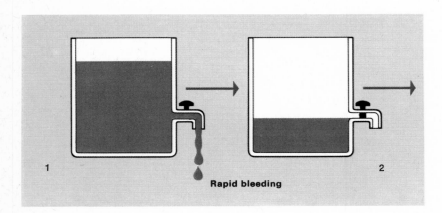

Rapid bleeding

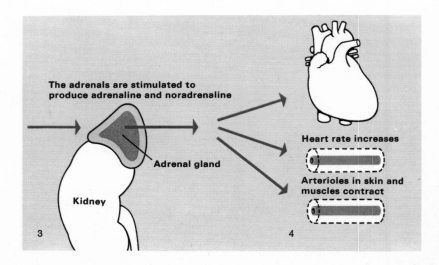

The adrenals are stimulated to produce adrenaline and noradrenaline

Adrenal gland

Kidney

Heart rate increases

Arterioles in skin and muscles contract

FAINTING

Fainting is a loss of consciousness caused by a temporary loss of blood supply to the brain. Getting out of bed for the first time after being ill for some time, standing in one position on parade, too many hot baths, too much tobacco, or a severe mental shock (which can be good news as well as bad) may all cause a faint. The main symptoms of fainting are a "sinking feeling", fuzzy vision, dim hearing, and a cold sweat. The person goes pale and sinks to the ground.

The blood in the veins is helped on its way back to the heart by the muscles in the limbs, especially the leg muscles. They squeeze the veins and act as a pump. If a person stays upright with no muscles at work his blood would pool in his legs. The heart can only pump out the blood circulated to it. If not enough reaches it, the heart may not be able to pump enough blood to the brain. So he faints. The result of a faint is falling to the ground. The body becomes horizontal, and in this position the flow of blood to the heart from the veins is improved. The heart pumps out its usual amount, the blood supply to the brain returns to normal and the patient recovers consciousness.

If someone feels he is going to faint, he should lie down or sit with his head between his knees until he feels better. But once a faint has happened, it is best to let the victim lie flat on his back with any tight clothing loosened. Do not force an unconscious person to drink.

The treatment after a shock is to make the patient lie flat with his legs raised so that his feet are higher than his head. This helps the blood to flow more easily to the brain, just as in a faint.

If there is severe loss of blood, a blood transfusion may be necessary to restore the blood pressure to its normal level.

Above: In this diagram, the red parts represent muscles contracting on a vein in order to push blood towards the heart through a vein valve. The lower valve closes to stop blood flowing back.

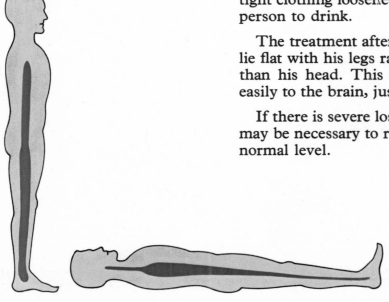

Left: Blood collects in the legs if a person stands for long. But if he faints, blood flows easily to the heart and brain since he is now lying flat.

THE BLOOD

The blood has liquid and solid parts. The liquid is *plasma*. The solid parts are the *red blood corpuscles*, *white blood corpuscles*, and *platelets*. An average-sized man has about 6 litres ($10\frac{1}{2}$ British pints) in his body. If he loses more than half of this he will die unless he has someone else's blood put into him by transfusion.

The blood carries water and food to every cell and takes waste products away. It carries oxygen from the lungs and carbon dioxide to them. It carries hormones from the glands, and antibodies to fight infection.

RED BLOOD CORPUSCLES

The red blood corpuscles carry oxygen, as is shown by the colour of blood. This is given by the pigment, *haemoglobin*, in the red corpuscles which pick up oxygen from the lungs and deliver it to the tissues. When carrying oxygen the blood is bright red. Without oxygen it is dark blue. "Blue babies" do not have enough oxygen in their blood.

In a drop of blood from a man there are about 5 million red corpuscles. A woman has about 4·5 million. There are far fewer white corpuscles – between 5 and 10 thousand – and half a million platelets.

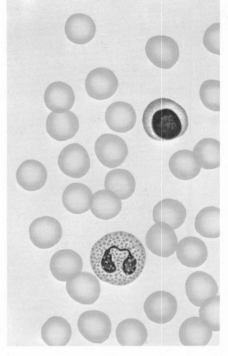

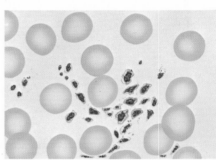

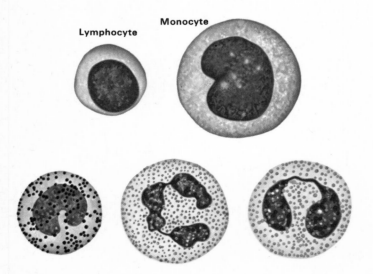

Lymphocyte

Monocyte

Above top: A sample of blood seen under a microscope. Most of the cells are red blood cells, but two are white cells.

Above: Another blood sample under the microscope to show red blood cells with a cluster of platelets.

Left: Five different types of white cell. The three at the bottom have granules in them and are the body's main defence against infection.

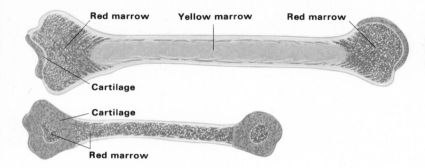

Red marrow   Yellow marrow   Red marrow

Cartilage

Cartilage

Red marrow

Left: This diagram of the bones of an adult (*top*) and a child (*bottom*) shows that red bone marrow fills more bone space in children than in adults.

All these parts of the blood take up almost half of its volume. The remainder consists of the blood plasma. Plasma is about 91 per cent water. Protein makes up the bulk of the remaining 9 per cent. Also in the plasma are salts, food, hormones, waste products, and antibodies.

Plasma is used for transfusion. The plasma part of blood is often as valuable as whole blood because plasma does not belong to any group (see Blood Groups) and it can be dried and stored.

BONE MARROW

In adults, the *bone marrow* makes the red cells, platelets, and most of the white cells. This jelly-like marrow is found in the centre of nearly all the bones. In young children this marrow is red and full of blood-forming cells. It gradually becomes yellow and contains a lot of fat. An adult has red marrow only in the spine, breastbone, ribs, pelvis, and skull. But the body can add to these stores by renewing the yellow marrow in the long bones (as in the arm and leg). So red marrow can be found in the centre of the thigh bones or the arm bones.

The new red and white cells and platelets are the final products of a series of primitive cells. These are of different shapes and sizes for the three types of grown-up cell.

There are only about 2½ gm of bone marrow in the body, and since there are millions of blood cells, and each has only a short life, (a red cell is thought to live for about 4 months) the marrow has to produce millions of fresh cells every day.

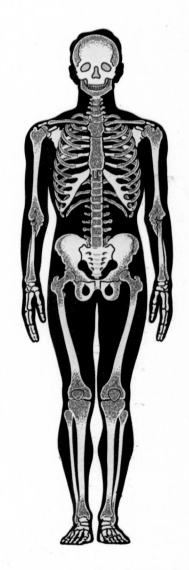

Above: In adult life the making of blood by the marrow is restricted to certain parts of the skeleton (marked red in this diagram). Doctors test bone marrow by taking a tiny amount from the breastbone with a special needle.

Above: This microscopic view is of granular white cells engulfing germs (the black dots) that have entered the body — in this case through a wound in the skin.

Right: Diagram to show how a lymph node is made. It is surrounded by an outer lining or cortex and has smaller nodules inside. *Efferent* lymph vessels are those taking lymph away. *Afferent* vessels are those bringing lymph in.

WHITE BLOOD CORPUSCLES

White cells are a different shape from red cells (see the illustration) and are of different types. They can move on their own (unlike the red cells which are pushed by the bloodstream) and do so along the sides of the blood vessels, rather than in the middle.

White cells are of two main types. The ones that, looked at under the microscope, have little grains in the substance surrounding the nucleus of the cell, and those that do not. Those showing the little grains are called *granular* cells.

The granular cells are the body's main defence against infection. In fact, they attack almost anything that enters the body from outside. They move towards a germ and gradually eat it by engulfing it. Then, inside the white cell the battle begins between the cell and the germ. Usually the white cell manages to kill the germ or germs. But when the poisons from a germ are too strong, the white cell dies. The yellowish matter called *pus* is largely made of many millions of dead granular white cells.

Inflammation, as in a boil, comes from more blood flowing to the infected area, and a leakage of cells and fluid in the infected area. These cause the redness and swelling.

When harmful germs invade the body, the bone

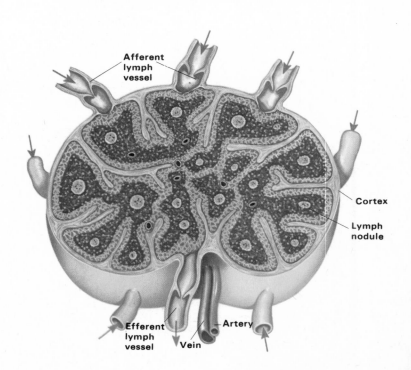

Afferent lymph vessel

Cortex

Lymph nodule

Efferent lymph vessel

Vein

Artery

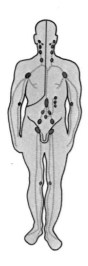

Above: A diagram of the human body to show the positions of the lymph nodes. They cluster together in little chains all over the body. They are usually near main arteries and veins.

Lymph nodes make *lymphocytes*, and lymph channels, long thin tubes, take them all over the body. The channels eventually drain into the main vein to the heart.

marrow produces more white cells to destroy them.

Of the *non-granular* cells, most are *lymphocytes*. They are made in the spleen and in the *lymph nodes*, which are found in chains, all over the body, but especially near the main blood vessels. Lymphocytes pass from the lymph nodes into lymph channels which eventually lead into the big vein that goes into the right atrium. Cells from the spleen go directly into the bloodstream and not into the lymph channels.

The lymph glands not only make lymphocytes but also act as a filter against infection entering the blood. For example, if a cut on the hand becomes infected, the lymph glands in the armpit become swollen and painful.

REJECTION PROCESSES

Besides the spleen and lymph nodes, there are several other tissues containing large amounts of lymphocytes. They include the tonsils and adenoids. When in contact with germs or other outside matter (such as transplanted tissues in a kidney transplant), lymphocytes increase in number and make antibodies in an effort to overcome the intruders. They are thus involved in the fight against infection and in the *rejection* process which takes place after spare-part surgery.

Monocytes, which make up a smaller number of the white cells in the blood, are like large lymphocytes. They eat foreign matter but are part of a different scavenging system. This system also includes similar cells in the connective tissues of the body, in the liver, the spleen and lymph nodes. They remove damaged or dead cells and foreign matter, and then destroy or store them.

The blood platelets are smaller than red or white blood cells, but there are more of them than white cells. They have no nucleus and are fragments of the marrow cells that produced them. Their main job is to help in the clotting of blood (see the chapter on Blood Clotting) and so help to stop bleeding.

The two main *plasma proteins* are substances called *albumin* and *globulin*. Albumin helps to keep fluid within the blood vessels and prevent it from accumulating in the tissues. It is largely formed in the liver. The globulin has a special part to play in fighting infection since it carries antibodies.

BLOOD GROUPS AND CLOTTING

A blood clot is the body's way of stopping bleeding. A plasma protein, *fibrinogen*, plays a vital part in this. Although only a small amount of it is in the blood, without it, bleeding would not stop.

BLEEDING AND CLOTTING

When bleeding starts, the blood flows for only a little while, less than five minutes. A cut, for example, soon becomes covered with a thick dark red mass, which is the blood clot. The platelets in the blood that flows from the cut, come into contact with the oxygen in the air and break up. A substance formed by the broken platelets works on certain other substances in the blood to alter the fibrinogen to *fibrin*.

Fibrin is like a spider's web made of minute threads that entangle platelets, red and white cells to make a blood clot. *Serum* is the name given to blood plasma without these clotting substances.

Clotting involves so many different processes that if one of the necessary parts is missing or is abnormal, blood will not clot properly. One of the diseases in which this happens is *haemophilia*. Small cuts and bruises bleed uncontrollably. This disease occurs almost entirely in males but is passed on by females.

BLOOD GROUPS

Everyone belongs to one of four blood groups, called A, B, AB, and O.

An Austrian doctor, Landsteiner, discovered three blood groups in 1900 and another one in 1902. There are other systems of blood groups (including the *rhesus* group) but the A, B, AB, O, system is by far the most important. Group O is sometimes called *universal* since it can nearly always be given to people of other groups.

In Great Britain, groups O and A are common (46 per cent and 42 per cent) while B (9 per cent) and AB (3 per cent) are rare.

Before a blood transfusion, it is important that the red blood cells being given are tested directly with

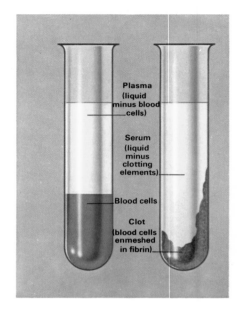

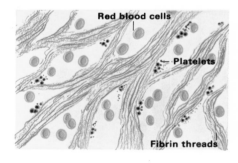

Above top: The tube on the left contains blood that has been treated to stop it clotting. It consists of blood cells and plasma. The tube on the right shows what happens if blood is left alone. Clotting elements separate from the plasma to enmesh the red and white blood cells and the platelets to form a clot. The liquid that is left is *serum*.

Above: A blood clot seen through a microscope. The threads of fibrin enmesh the red and white cells and platelets.

Right: A chart showing how *haemophilia* (the "bleeding disease") is inherited. Females pass it on, but it is the males who inherit it, with very few exceptions. In this case only one boy has inherited it.

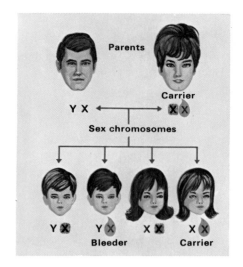

Below: A Rhesus baby's blood is incompatible with its mother's. At birth, its blood will need replacing by transfusion to save its life.

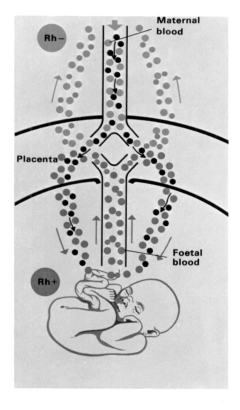

the serum of the recipient. If the cells mix with the serum without "clumping", the blood transfusion will be *compatible*. But if the cells clump together, the transfusion will be *incompatible*.

Transfusion of incompatible blood may kill the recipient because the capillary blood vessels may become blocked with clumped red cells and block the blood flow to the vital organs, particularly the kidneys. Over a million bottles of blood or plasma are used for transfusion every year in England and Wales. It is needed especially when multiple accidents occur.

PLASMA

Plasma is blood without red and white cells. It is the best known substitute for blood because it can be stored and transported easily. Blood banks hold stores of plasma for use in blood transfusions.

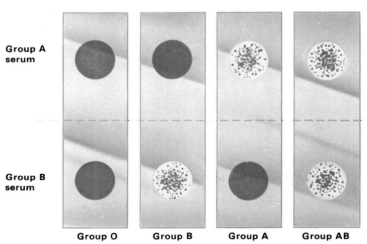

Right: The first step in a blood transfusion is to test the blood of both the donor and recipient against serum A or B. The yellow circles show which samples are incompatible.

BREATHING

Breathing provides the body, through the lungs, with oxygen, and removes the used air from it, which contains a high proportion of carbon dioxide. Every cell needs oxygen for energy. Carbon dioxide, a gas, is formed during this process, but it has to be removed or else it will poison the cells.

VENTILATION

Passing air in and out of the lungs is called *ventilation*. Most of this work is done by a muscle called the *diaphragm* which is dome-shaped and lies between the chest and the abdomen. Muscles between the ribs also help.

The lungs are encased in a thin membrane called the pluera. This two-layered structure enables the lungs to move freely without them rubbing against the chest wall.

Just before breath is drawn in, the pressure inside the lungs is the same as the pressure of the air outside.

Opposite page: A man breathing in (*top*). His ribs rise up and outwards, his diaphragm moves downwards to make the chest bigger. When he breathes out (*bottom*), the diaphragm moves up and the ribs down and in. So the chest space is smaller because the lungs are no longer full.

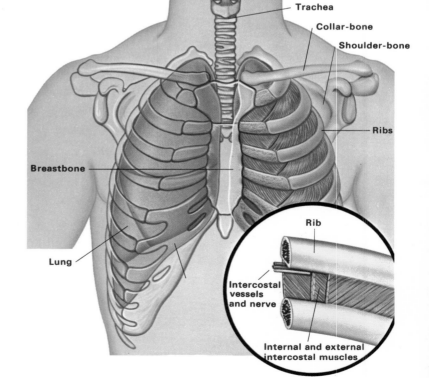

Trachea

Collar-bone

Shoulder-bone

Ribs

Breastbone

Lung

Rib

Intercostal vessels and nerve

Internal and external intercostal muscles

Right: This is a model of the front of the chest. On the left the lung can be seen through the ribs. On the right, the ribs and the muscles between the ribs cover the lungs. The circle inset shows the intercostal muscles (intercostal means "between the ribs"). They are in two layers, outer and inner, with nerves and blood vessels next to them.

Right: The diagram shows front and back views of the lungs, and the many-branched air passages. Each tube (bronchus) serves a different part of the lung. (The tubes and parts of the lungs are marked with corresponding numbers).

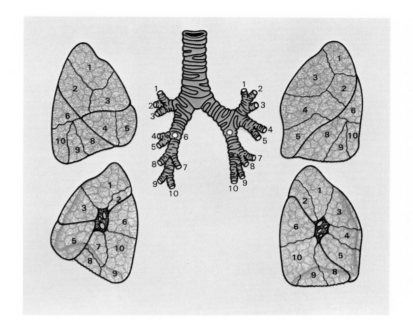

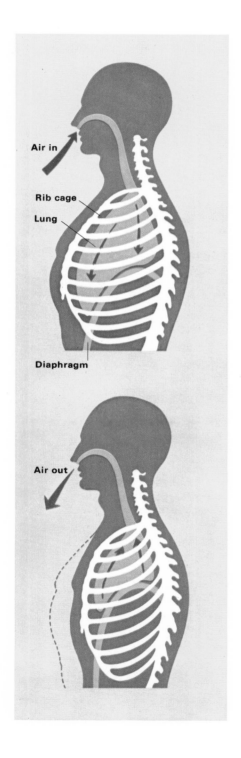

Then the muscles between the ribs contract and move all the ribs up and outwards. Simultaneously the diaphragm contracts and moves downwards. Because of these muscle movements the size of the chest increases and the air pressure inside the chest falls. Since Nature always balances pressures, outside air comes into the chest to make the pressure inside the same as that outside.

After breathing in, the muscles relax. They go back to the position they were in before the start of taking a breath. The size of the space in which the lungs lie diminishes. This fall in the cavity's capacity, together with the natural elasticity of the lungs, forces the air, now rich in carbon dioxide, out of the lungs and back into the outside world.

THE AIR PASSAGES

Air is made up of about 20 per cent oxygen and 79 per cent nitrogen. It enters the body through the mouth and nose. Then it goes through the throat into the main airway, the *trachea*. This is a firm tube that can be felt at the front of the neck. In the chest, the trachea divides into two tubes. These are the *bronchi*. The air is now in the chest and can go to the right or left lungs (a pair weigh about one kg and the right lung is slightly larger than the left).

The bronchi now divide into smaller and smaller branches and their smallest branches which are very minute (a few thousandths of a millimetre wide) open into spaces called *alveoli*.

45

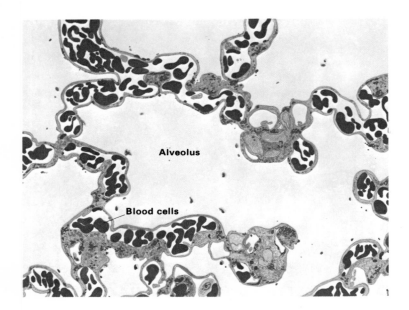

Left: An alveolus seen through a microscope. The air in the alveolus goes through the thin barrier between it and the blood cells. The blood cells take in oxygen and give up carbon dioxide.

Alveolus

Blood cells

Below: A diagram showing a group of alveoli and their blood supply. Here, oxygen passes into the blood.

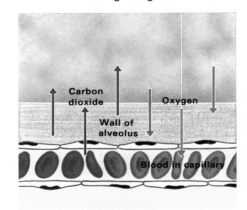

Carbon dioxide   Oxygen

Deoxygenated blood   Oxygenated blood

Below: Cross-section of the alveolus wall showing the closeness of blood and air in the lungs. During exercise the blood takes only one third of a second to exchange its gases.

Carbon dioxide   Oxygen

Wall of alveolus

Blood in capillary

THE EXCHANGE OF GASES

Alveoli are lined by a single layer of cells lying on very thin tissue which contains the tiniest blood vessels (capillaries). The barrier between the air in the alveoli and the capillaries, in other words between the air from outside and the blood, is minute, no more than a thousandth of a millimetre thick.

There are a great number of the alveoli as they are very important. They cover an area forty to fifty times that of the skin on the surface of the body. But each capillary in them is only wide enough to let pass one red cell at a time. That time lasts three-quarters of a second. This is very short, but long enough for the cell to give up its carbon dioxide and take up its share of oxygen.

The pumping of the blood through the alveoli is done by the heart. A grown man has about six litres of air in his lungs. He breathes only about half a litre in and out when just going about quietly. But a big breath in followed by a big breath out will push out four to five litres of air. Doctors use this *vital capacity* as a mark of the lungs' health. Athletes can breathe out more air, and old people less. Smoking just one cigarette can reduce the capacity.

CONTROL OF BREATHING

Breathing is controlled by a group of special nerve cells in the part of the brain called the medulla. These

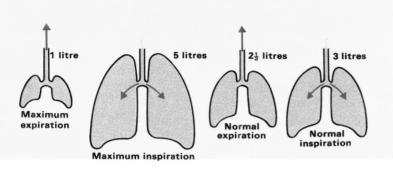

Left: This shows the capacity of the lungs during normal breathing (*left*) and during deep breathing (*far left*). (Expiration means breathing out; inspiration means breathing in.)

cells are sensitive to the nerve information sent back to them from the lungs, and also to the amount of oxygen and carbon dioxide in the blood.

Breathing can become difficult if the human body is away from the pressure in the atmosphere that it is used to. This is felt most often when travelling by air or climbing a high mountain. Aircraft cabins are "pressurized" so that the passengers do not suffer, but climbing in "thin" air (air without the amount of pressure at sea level) needs getting used to. Everest was climbed with the help of oxygen breathing apparatus.

ARTIFICIAL RESPIRATION

Failure of breathing will occur when the lungs cannot do their job of giving oxygen to the blood and carrying the carbon dioxide away.

You may find yourself the only person nearby when someone is in need of help in breathing – such as after electric shock or near-drowning. There are several methods of *artificial respiration* but the one everybody should know how to perform is the *mouth-to-mouth* method, also known as the "kiss of life". It is simple and works well.

See first that the victim's mouth is clear of any obstruction (seaweed, perhaps, or false teeth) and then lie him flat on his back. His head should be tipped back and his lower jaw forced forward. This prevents his tongue falling back and blocking the airway. The rescuer breathes in deeply, and then, while holding the victim's nose, he puts his mouth over the victim's and breathes out fully. He then allows the victim to breathe out. He repeats this action twenty times a minute (about the normal rate of breathing) until the victim begins to breathe again.

Below: Mouth-to-mouth resuscitation. The victim's head is tilted well back to make sure the airway is clear.

Below bottom: First-aid treatment for a stopped heart. This method is known as external heart massage. With one palm on the bottom of the breast-bone, place the other palm over it and press firmly up and down until the heart begins to beat.

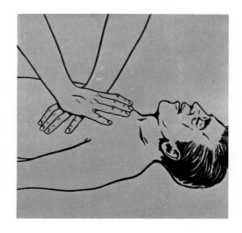

FOOD AND THE DIGESTIVE SYSTEM

Food is made of *proteins*, *carbohydrates*, *fats*, *salts*, *vitamins* and water. The body needs them all to keep healthy. Proteins, carbohydrates, and fats have to be altered by *digestion* before the body can use them.

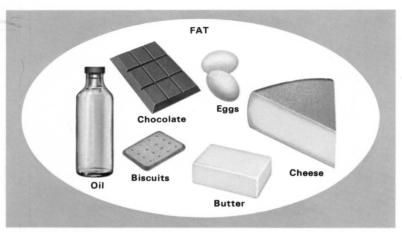

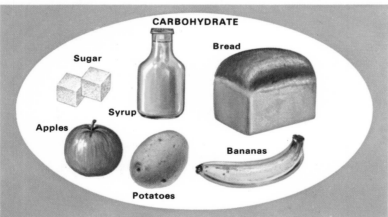

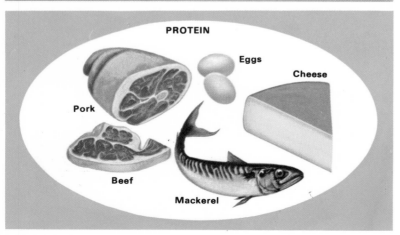

Left: The main groups of food: fat, carbohydrate and protein, represented here by some of the everyday items in a western diet, grouped under their main content. They are not all made of one main group only. Cheese, for instance, contains fat and protein. Most of the energy supply begins as carbohydrate, though sugar is now thought to be too popular in diets. Over half the British people are said to be overweight through eating too much.

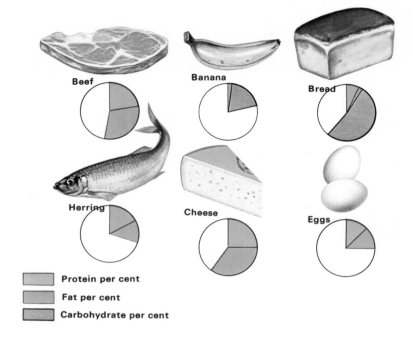

Right: This diagram shows what proportions of the three main food groups are present in meat, fruit, bread, fish, cheese and eggs. They all contain some protein and everything except the fruit contains some fat. The fruit and bread contain carbohydrates. All the items contain a large amount of water (represented by the white area).

Beef

Banana

Bread

Herring

Cheese

Eggs

Protein per cent

Fat per cent

Carbohydrate per cent

The breaking down of these foods and the building up of body tissue is called *metabolism*. In metabolism, energy is released to maintain vital processes such as breathing, blood circulation, kidney and brain function. Energy release, and the making of food into chemicals that the cells can use, goes on all the time.

CARBOHYDRATE, PROTEIN AND FAT

Carbohydrates form most of the food you eat. They are made of carbon, hydrogen and oxygen, and are *sugars* and *starch*. All carbohydrates, wherever they come from, are turned into glucose. They are the body's chief source of energy.

Proteins are the body builders. They are the basic material of living cells. Protein is made by green plants, and this is eaten by humans or by animals that humans eat. When we eat meat, the plant protein has already been changed into protein in the meat, which is animal muscle. Proteins are made of many *amino acids* (chains of carbon, hydrogen, oxgyen and nitrogen linked together chemically).

Fats act as a shock absorber under the skin and around vulnerable organs like the kidneys, but they are also a concentrated energy store. Fats are made of *fatty acids* and *glycerol*.

MINERAL SALTS

Carbohydrates, fats and proteins contain enough of the carbon, hydrogen, oxygen, nitrogen and sulphur that are essential for life. But the body also needs very small amounts of other elements. These are the *mineral salts*. They include *cobalt*, *copper* and *molybdenum*. *Sodium* and *potassium* are vital in the body fluids. *Calcium* and *phosphate* are for making bone,

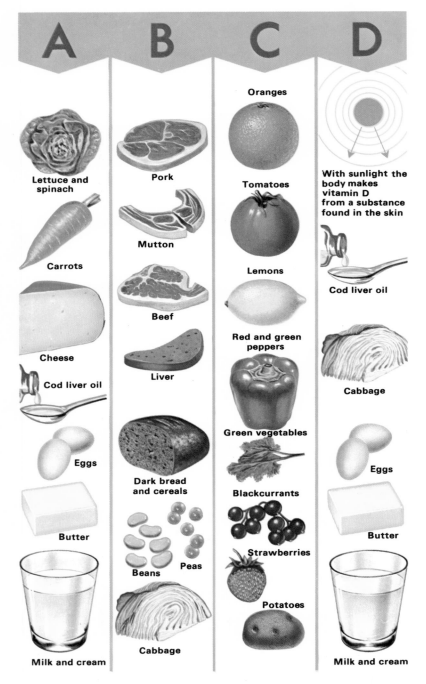

A

Lettuce and spinach

Carrots

Cheese

Cod liver oil

Eggs

Butter

Milk and cream

B

Pork

Mutton

Beef

Liver

Dark bread and cereals

Beans   Peas

Cabbage

C

Oranges

Tomatoes

Lemons

Red and green peppers

Green vegetables

Blackcurrants

Strawberries

Potatoes

D

With sunlight the body makes vitamin D from a substance found in the skin

Cod liver oil

Cabbage

Eggs

Butter

Milk and cream

Left: Some sources of the principal vitamins. Vitamin A is stored in the liver. Too little of it may cause thickening and dryness of the skin, and night blindness. Vitamin B is a group of vitamins. Among diseases caused by lack of it are beri-beri and pellagra. Vitamin C is essential for repair of tissues. It helps wounds heal. Patients lacking it bruise easily and their gums swell and bleed. Full lack of vitamin C causes the disease of scurvy. Vitamin D is essential for forming bone. A child with a lack of vitamin D will develop rickets.

Iron for haemoglobin, and *iodine* goes into thyroid hormones.

Minerals do not provide the body with energy. They replace minerals lost from the body in day-to-day wear and tear. The growing body also needs them to build with, not just to replace themselves.

VITAMINS

Even with all these carbohydrates, fats, proteins, and minerals, the human body still needs more. It needs *vitamins*.

There are about 40 vitamins but only about 12 are needed for health. They can be divided into two groups; the ones that dissolve in water, and the ones that dissolve in fat. Whatever group a vitamin belongs to, the daily amounts needed are very, very small – measured in tenths of a milligram.

Vitamins are very important. If a body does not get enough of them the processes that go on in each cell to convert the food chemicals into living matter, run down, or even stop. Vitamin deficiencies affect the body in many ways.

DIGESTION

Digestion is the way the body changes food so that the blood can absorb and carry it to the cells. All body cells live on this nourishment.

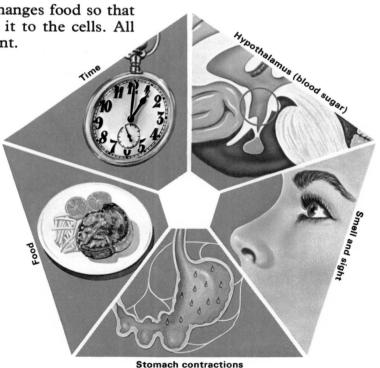

Time

Hypothalamus (blood sugar)

Smell and sight

Food

Stomach contractions

Right: This diagram shows some of the things that affect the appetite. They include the look, smell and taste of food. The amount of sugar in the blood is important. Too little stimulates the brain centre responsible for appetite control to increase appetite. People who have regular meal times find themselves getting into the habit of feeling hunger pains due to stomach contractions, at the times at which they expect to be fed.

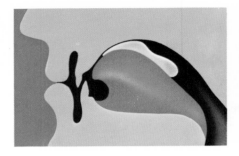

Digestion begins in the mouth. The teeth break up food, the *saliva* (spit) wets it, and the *tongue* mixes it to make it easy to swallow. An adult produces about $1\frac{1}{2}$ litres of saliva a day.

THE TEETH

There are 32 permanent teeth in the mouth of a man or woman, sixteen in the upper jaw and sixteen in the lower. They are of three different types: (1) the *incisors* that cut the food, (2) the *canines* that tear it, and (3) the *molars* that grind it.

Enamel, the hardest substance in the body, covers the outside of a tooth. The centre is a soft *pulp*, which contains blood vessels and nerves. Between the pulp and the enamel is a harder substance called *dentine*. The part of the tooth above the *gum* is the *crown*. The *neck* of a tooth is covered by the gum, and the *root* lies in the tooth socket in the jawbone.

Before the food is even swallowed digestion has already begun. Saliva in the mouth creates a chemical change in any starch the food contains so that it becomes a sugar.

Above: The tongue (in red) is seen here mixing and moulding food into a lump (bolus) for easy swallowing. Nerve endings in the back of the mouth and throat set off a chain of complicated movements each time something is swallowed.

Opposite page: The top diagram shows food being moved along the digestive canal by peristalsis. In the stomach (*bottom picture*) gastric juices are poured out in response to a signal from the brain. They break down food so that the body can absorb it.

Left: The diagram showing how a lump of food progresses from the mouth into the gullet. The tongue plays the main part, pushing it to the back of the throat, where the swallowing reflex takes over.

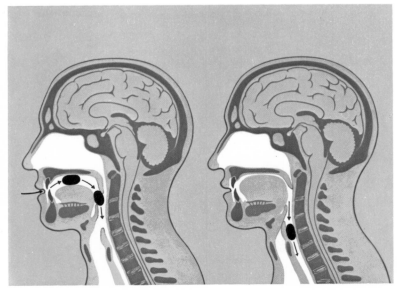

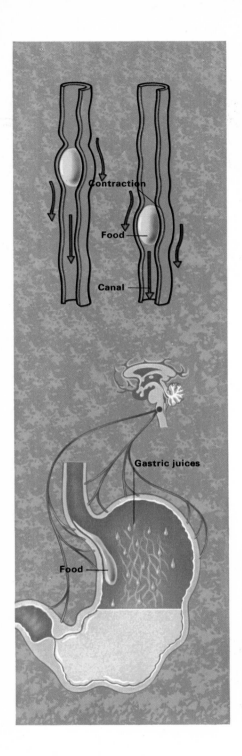

SWALLOWING

A mouthful of food then passes backwards into the throat. It is the start of a long journey in which food moves along a continuous channel about nine metres long known as the *alimentary canal*. This canal begins at the mouth and includes the gullet (*oesophagus*), the *stomach*, the *small intestine* and the *large intestine*.

When food enters the gullet, *peristalsis* begins: slow automatic contractions occur along the entire length of the alimentary canal propelling the contents onward. Peristalsis in the gullet is so efficient that liquids will enter the stomach even if a person is upside down.

THE STOMACH

The stomach is a muscular bag which churns the food and pours *digestive juices* onto it. These digestive juices begin the digestion of the protein part of food. Food stays in the stomach for two to four hours before it moves into the small intestine (called small because it is narrower than the large intestine). The greater part of digestion occurs here. In the small intestine, more juices which include juices from the pancreas, and the bile from the liver, finish digestion of carbohydrates and proteins and break down the fats. This takes about five hours.

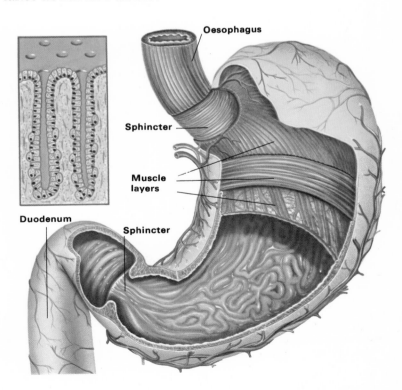

Right: The stomach. At entrance and exit is a *sphincter*, (a muscle surrounding a tube to open or close it). At the exit is the *duodenum*, the first part of the small intestine. Inset is a small picture showing the stomach lining (magnified).

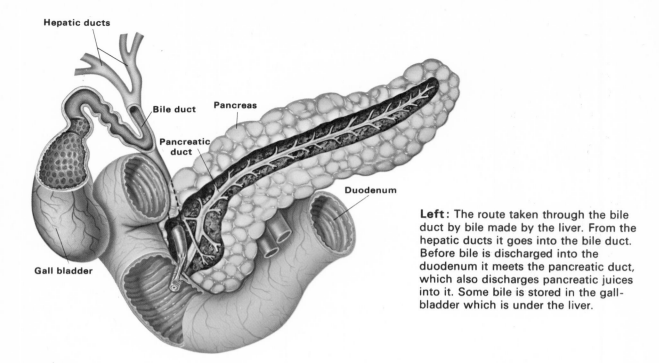

Hepatic ducts

Bile duct

Pancreas

Pancreatic duct

Duodenum

Gall bladder

Left: The route taken through the bile duct by bile made by the liver. From the hepatic ducts it goes into the bile duct. Before bile is discharged into the duodenum it meets the pancreatic duct, which also discharges pancreatic juices into it. Some bile is stored in the gall-bladder which is under the liver.

THE ALIMENTARY CANAL

Nearly all digested food passes through the lining of the intestines into the blood. The inner lining of the small intestine has a number of projections, called *villi*, that absorb the food and pass it into the tiny blood vessels inside them. Once in the bloodstream,

Right: The contents of the abdomen seen from the front. The small intestine is about 6 metres long, the large about 2 metres.

The appendix is a blind tube which opens off the first part of the large intestine. Appendicitis is the name given to inflammation of this organ.

The liver is the largest organ in the body and has many jobs to do. It stores carbohydrates, fats, and proteins. It makes bile, which helps absorb fats from the intestines. It contains vitamin B_{12} for the growth of red blood cells, and it destroys red blood cells, too. It deals with drugs and poisons that get into the body. In an adult the liver weighs about $1\frac{1}{2}$ kg.

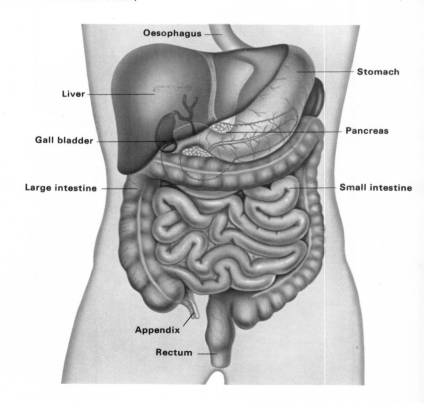

Oesophagus

Stomach

Liver

Pancreas

Gall bladder

Large intestine

Small intestine

Appendix

Rectum

all digested carbohydrate, protein and 40 per cent of fats go to the liver, which converts them into a form the body can easily use. It stores vitamins A and D. Those parts of the food that are not digested (because the body does not need them) go through the two-metre-long large intestine to its lowest part, the *rectum*. This waste goes out through the *anus*, the opening of the lower end of the alimentary canal, about 24 hours after food has been eaten.

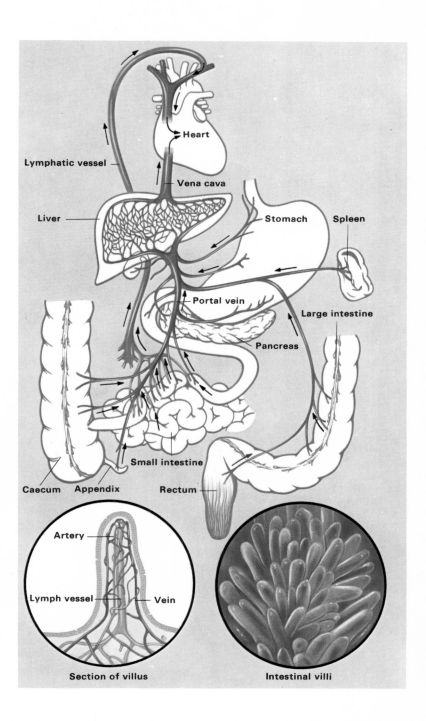

Right: This diagram shows the system of vessels that carry the digested food from the intestines. The green coloured tubes represent the lymphatic system which carries fats from the intestines into the blood. (*Inset left*) the position of a lymph vessel in the villus. (*Inset right*) intestinal villi, the fingerlike projections, hardly visible to the naked eye, that line the small intestines. Other food digested is absorbed by the blood vessels of the villi.

DIET

The diet means the variety of food a person eats. It varies from one group of people to another and from country to country and race to race.

Food has to provide enough water, calories, minerals, and vitamins if a person is to be healthy.

Water makes up 70 per cent of the human body. Some is lost through the kidneys, and further amounts in the breath, sweat, and waste from the intestines. This water has to be replaced.

All life needs energy. This comes from a continuous supply of food. Even during sleep, the heart, lungs, kidneys and liver go on working. So do the muscles and brain.

CALORIES

During sleep the body needs about 500 calories as fuel. A *calorie* is a measure of the fuel capacity of food. The more active the body is, the more energy (calories) it needs. As the illustration shows, writing at a desk uses 40 to 50 calories an hour, light housework needs 100 to 150 calories and heavy work like road-digging uses up to 300 calories an hour.

Right: The map shows how diets vary round the world. The world is short of protein and lack of it is the greatest single cause of malnutrition. Protein made in a laboratory is likely to form part of most people's diet in the future. The figures given (*encircled*) represent the following: (*top*) average daily calorie intake, (*middle*) proportion of calories derived from carbohydrates: (*bottom*) daily intake of protein measured in grams.

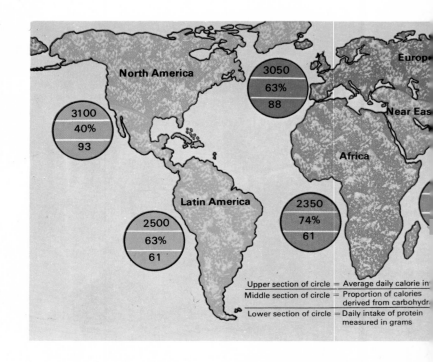

North America

3050
63%
88

Europe

3100
40%
93

Near East

Africa

Latin America

2500
63%
61

2350
74%
61

Upper section of circle = Average daily calorie in
Middle section of circle = Proportion of calories derived from carbohydr
Lower section of circle = Daily intake of protein measured in grams

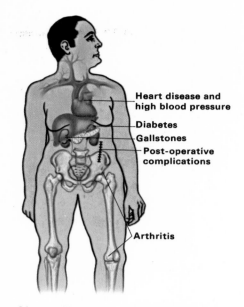

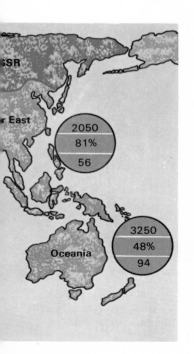

Above: This man shows some of the bad effects of being too fat. Post-operative complications are the problems that arise in the body after a surgical operation. There is a greater risk of them occurring in fat people.

For sport, about 150 calories an hour are needed for a gentle game of tennis, but up to 900 calories an hour for a hard game of squash.

Each person's needs are different. Growing children use up a lot of calories.

HOW OTHERS EAT

Before talking about a normal western diet, it helps to see how the rest of the world eats. Perhaps as many as half the people in the world do not get enough to eat. They do not have sufficient food to give them enough calories, and they may not get the necessary amount of protein and vitamins in what they do eat. A child who does not get enough to eat grows up stunted, without much resistance to infectious diseases such as measles, whooping-cough and tuberculosis.

The food problem in western civilization is eating too much. More than half the people in Britain are probably overweight. This is serious because *obesity*, the name doctors give to this state, shortens life, and leads to disease. If a person takes in more food (more calories) than he needs, he will gain weight. There are some people who seem to be able to eat all they want to and still not put on weight. It seems probable that they have a much higher rate of burning up food than other people have. However, most fat people are simply people who eat and drink too much.

The number of calories a man or woman or child needs is lower today than it used to be. Mr Standard Man needs about 2750 calories, Mrs Standard Woman about 2250. A child of 12 needs almost as much.

A reasonable diet should contain at least 60 gm of protein daily and carbohydrate and fat to provide the bulk of calorie needs. But most people eat carbohydrate, protein and fat in the proportion 4:1:1.

Bread and potatoes provide most of the carbohydrate calories, followed by sugar and cereals. Butter, margarine, oil, lard, and dripping, provide more energy weight-for-weight than carbohydrates and also help to make starchy foods nicer to eat even though they themselves may not be appetising alone. Protein is essential for building new tissues. Protein is provided mainly by meat and dairy produce such as eggs, cheese and milk.

Diet is important in the care of people who suffer from certain diseases, such as diabetes. All big hospitals have dietiticians on their staff to plan special diets for patients who need them.

In Western countries, the average person does not need to worry about his diet too much. He is unlikely to be short of any vital ingredient unless he is very poor or deliberately eating special food, but there are some exceptions. Old people living alone may not be eating the right sort of food and some of them do not get enough vitamins. Women who are pregnant need extra food of various sorts to provide for the growing baby inside them. Growing children need more of some food substances than an adult. For example, they need extra calcium for their growing bones.

Above: A boy working at a desk uses 40 calories an hour, a girl doing housework uses about 125 calories, a tennis player uses about 500 calories.

Above: The body uses energy all the time. Even when a person is asleep, sitting in a car, just talking on the telephone, or trying to keep perfectly still and relaxed, he or she is burning up calories. The nervous system and all the vital body functions require fuel from food to keep them functioning.

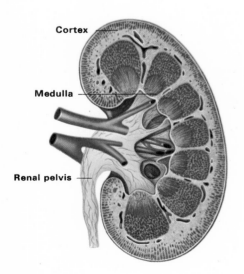

THE KIDNEYS

The human body has two kidneys. But a few people are born with only one. The two kidneys are not exactly the same size and shape. The left kidney is not as wide as the right kidney, and is a little longer. Both kidneys lie in the abdomen on its back wall on either side of the spine, just below the diaphragm. The left kidney is a little higher than the right.

Each kidney weighs about 150 gm and is about 10 cm long. Blood comes to the kidney by a large artery that branches off from the aorta. This artery divides into three smaller arteries when it enters the kidney. The veins in the kidney unite to form one big vein that returns the blood from the kidney to the main vein leading to the right side of the heart.

URINE

Urine is made in the kidneys. It collects in a funnel-shaped, thin-walled part of the kidney called the *renal pelvis*. This leads into a tube called the *ureter*, which leads into the *bladder* lower down in the abdomen. The ureter contracts in slow waves to help the urine pass from the kidney to the bladder.

An average man makes up to $1\frac{1}{2}$ litres of urine a day (24 hours) and the bladder can easily hold half a litre. When a man wants to pass urine, his grey matter in the brain sends the message to a tight muscle guarding the exit from the bladder and it relaxes. Then the muscle in the wall of the bladder contracts and pushes out the urine.

If a kidney is cut in half (as in the picture) an outer part, the *cortex*, and an inner part, the *medulla*, can be seen. The cortex contains many nests of tiny blood vessels leading into coiled tubes which partly lie in the medulla. Each nest of blood vessels and its tube is called a *nephron*. Through this system the kidney excretes waste. Each kidney has about $1\frac{1}{2}$ million nephrons.

THE WORK OF THE KIDNEYS

The most important job that the kidneys do is to remove waste products and to form urine. They also regulate the amount of salt and fluid in the body and see that the body fluids are kept slightly alkaline (and not acid).

Above: The urinary system. The adrenal glands are not part of it, but are attached to the kidneys.

Below: Cross-section of a kidney to show the outer cortex and the inner medulla.

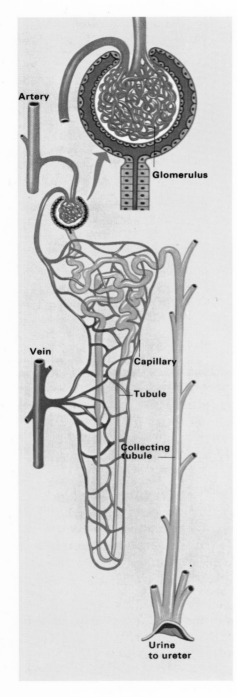

The waste products have to be removed because they poison the cells if they stay in the body. The fats and carbohydrates in the food can be broken down to form carbon dioxide and water. The carbon dioxide is excreted through the lungs (together with about half a litre of water a day).

The kidneys have to deal with the waste products of the protein in the food, especially the nitrogen that is part of protein. This nitrogen is formed into *urea* by the body. The amount of urea excreted in the urine is about 30 gm a day. When urine is analyzed, it should be found to contain 2 per cent of urea, 95 per cent water, 1 per cent common salt, and 2 per cent of other substances that the body does not want. The yellow colour of urine is due to pigments, but if a lot of fluid is drunk the colour becomes paler. A number of diseases can change the colour of urine; so can eating certain foods. Beetroot, some sweets, as well as some drugs, can alter its colour.

CONTROL OF BODY FLUIDS

All this work is done by the nephrons. About a litre of blood is pumped through the kidneys by the heart every minute. It is filtered by the nephrons and they remove the waste products the body does not want. They also return to the blood, through the tubes leading to the pelvis, substances that the body needs such as water and glucose.

In this way the kidneys control the body fluids. The liquid that now begins its journey to the bladder as urine, is acid. The kidneys see to it that the amount of water they allow to leave the body in the urine is

Above: a *nephron*, the excretory unit of the kidney. The filter action of each nephron is begun by a glomerulus. This is a tiny bunch of blood vessels.

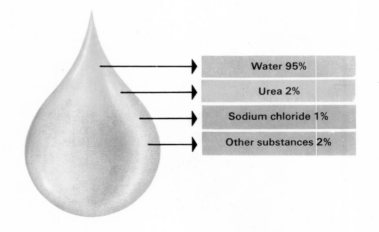

Right: The normal constituents of urine. The state of the urine is a valuable guide to a person's health.

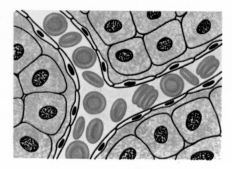

Right: Human bodies are made mostly of water. It carries chemicals, and it cools the body. Water forms a large part of all food and drink. Man will die after a few days without water. This diagram shows where the water in the body is at any given time. 30 litres are in the cells, 12 litres between the cells and 3 litres in the bloodstream.

The diagram (*above*) shows where the water is distributed in the cells.

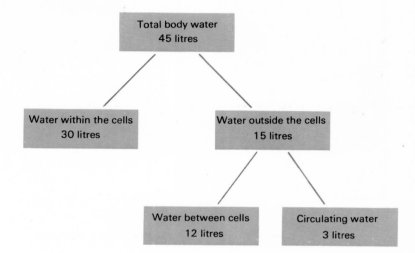

not only sufficient to dissolve the waste products it contains but also leaves sufficient water in the body to allow all the bodily functions to act properly.

The body fluids that the kidneys look after are formed mostly of water. Water accounts for two-thirds of total body weight. An average-sized man contains about 45 litres of water.

This water is spread throughout the body. About 30 litres is within the cells. It helps keep their size and shape correct, and acts as a fluid store in which are food, oxygen, and waste products.

About three litres of water are in the heart and blood vessels. Together with the red and white cells, it forms the bulk of the blood, about six litres. The rest of the body water, about 12 litres, lies in the space between the body cells.

The kidneys are able to keep all this water in the body. If the fluid passing through a kidney all the time were to be excreted, the water in the blood would be lost within half an hour.

As well as water, the kidneys look after the *salts* dissolved in it. The most important are sodium, chlorine, potassium, calcium, and phosphate. These are all kept at the right level in the blood by the kidneys.

Water lost in urine and faeces	Water lost in breathing	Water lost in sweating

Right: An average man loses about 2½ litres of water a day. Nearly 1½ litres is lost from urine and waste (faeces) from the digestive tract. Just over half a litre is lost as sweat and about half a litre is expelled from the lungs.

KIDNEY MACHINES AND TRANSPLANTS

When the kidney cannot do its work, this is called *kidney failure*. The work can be taken over by a *kidney machine*.

Kidney transplants are now performed all over the world to replace kidneys that cannot function properly. The patient is usually kept on a kidney machine until a suitable kidney can be found from another person. Although it is not hard for a surgeon to transplant a kidney, the problem of *rejection* is not yet fully solved. The best results have come when the person receiving a kidney is a close relative of the person giving it.

Left: A diagram to show how the artificial kidney works. Two or three times a week the patient is connected to a machine for several hours while his blood is "washed" by being put through a coiled tube immersed in a bath of special, sterile fluid. The blood comes from an artery and is pumped back into a vein.

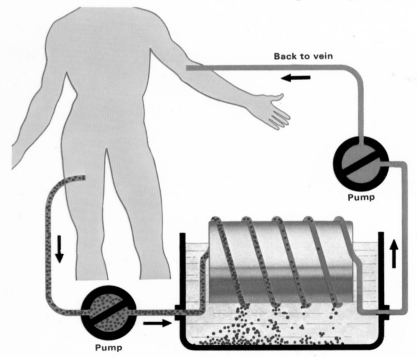

Back to vein

Pump

Pump

GLANDS AND HORMONES

In the human body are glands, each a collection of special cells, that manufacture substances that pass directly into the bloodstream. These are carried in the blood all over the body, and take effect far from the glands themselves. The substances are called *hormones*. There are about thirty of them, from eight different glands. Because these glands send their products directly into the bloodstream, and not through any special channel or duct, these glands are called the "ductless glands".

Some hormones can now be made in the laboratory. Even small amounts of hormones are very powerful. They control growth, sexual activity, pregnancy, birth, and metabolism.

Right: The endocrine glands of a woman. These are ductless glands that secrete hormones directly into the bloodstream. In the pancreas there are cells that make insulin. Part of the ovary makes the hormone progesterone. This hormone prepares the lining of the uterus to nourish the fertilized egg.

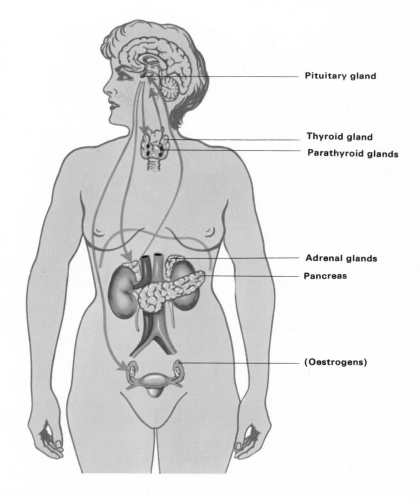

Pituitary gland

Thyroid gland
Parathyroid glands

Adrenal glands
Pancreas

(Oestrogens)

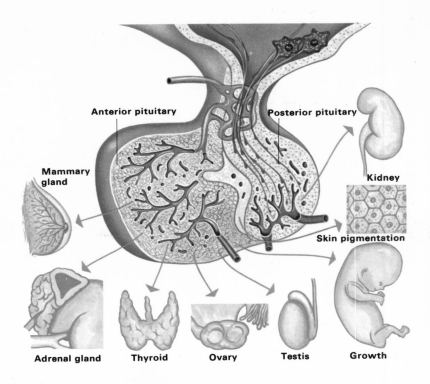

Anterior pituitary

Posterior pituitary

Mammary gland

Kidney

Skin pigmentation

Adrenal gland

Thyroid

Ovary

Testis

Growth

THE PITUITARY GLAND

Most hormone-making is under the control of a gland called the pituitary, the size of a hazel nut, lying in a little hollow in the middle of the bottom of the skull. The front part of the pituitary makes about half a dozen hormones that go in the blood to other glands, to stimulate them into making hormones. These hormones then circulate in the blood, back round to the pituitary. If too much has been manufactured, the pituitary damps down its stimulus.

Glands dependent on this pituitary secretion are the *adrenals*, the *thyroid*, and the *sex glands*. If the pituitary is damaged, these glands cannot make their own hormones properly.

The back part of the pituitary stores two hormones produced in a nearby part of the brain called the *hypothalamus*. One of these two hormones make the kidney absorb water from the urine. The other hormone makes the muscles of the womb contract during childbirth, and stimulates the breasts to give milk to feed the new-born baby.

THE ADRENAL GLANDS

The *adrenal glands* have two parts with different functions. There is an outer part (*cortex*) and an inner (*medulla*). The two adrenals are yellow-brown

Above: The pituitary gland is often called "the leader of the endocrine orchestra" since it controls the activity of the other ductless glands. This diagram shows its range of influence. The pituitary gland is about the size of a hazel nut and is connected to the under surface of the brain by a stalk through which it receives its nerve supply. Its importance is out of all proportion to its size.

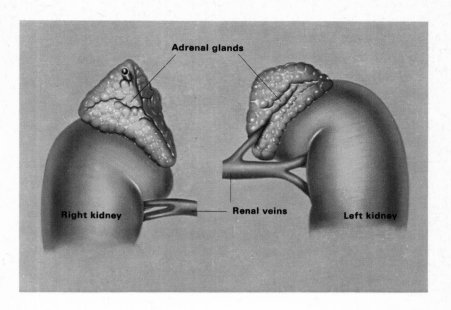

Adrenal glands

Right kidney

Renal veins

Left kidney

triangles near the upper ends of the kidneys. They weigh about seven gm each. The medulla produces two hormones, *adrenaline* and *noradrenaline*. These hormones act with the part of the nervous system known as the *sympathetic nervous system*. This is part of what is known as the *autonomic nervous system*, which controls the involuntary muscles (see page 13). These include the muscles found in the heart, blood vessels, intestines, bladder and other organs. They produce a faster pulse, a raised blood pressure, a wide pupil, more sugar in the blood – all actions of the body designed to help the body in "fight or flight". This is why skin goes pale and forms "goose-flesh" when a person is frightened.

Above: The two adrenal glands. They are shown here as they lie in the body, one on the top of each kidney to which it is attached.

Left: The outer part of the adrenal gland makes a number of hormones that are essential to life. These are the corticosteroids. Some of the functions the adrenal controls are shown here. Corticotrophin is made by the pituitary gland and it uses it to stimulate the adrenal gland to make more corticosteroids when needed. Adrenaline is made by the medulla of the adrenal gland.

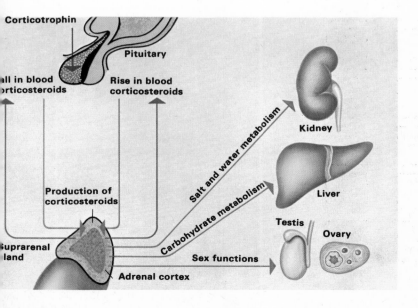

Corticotrophin

Pituitary

Fall in blood corticosteroids

Rise in blood corticosteroids

Production of corticosteroids

Salt and water metabolism

Kidney

Carbohydrate metabolism

Liver

Testis

Ovary

Suprarenal gland

Sex functions

Adrenal cortex

INSULIN AND DIABETES

Insulin is the hormone made by the pancreas. A lack of insulin causes diabetes. Insulin was discovered in 1922 by Drs Banting and Best. Tiny cells in the pancreas between the glands that pour out pancreatic juice for digestion, make the insulin. The chief effect of insulin is to lower the amount of sugar (glucose) in the blood. To do this it makes the liver and muscles store sugar, it pushes more glucose into cells to break it down into water and carbon dioxide, and it makes more fat.

Without enough insulin, the whole metabolism of the body is upset, but the immediate result is too much glucose in the blood. This appears in the urine. Fat in the body is also broken down too much, and the sugar in the urine also takes a lot of water with it.

An untreated diabetic is thin and dry with sugar in the urine. Before insulin was discovered, diabetes was always fatal. Today a diabetic can lead a reasonable life. A diabetic usually injects himself with one of the many different sorts of insulin, and this becomes a habit he gets used to.

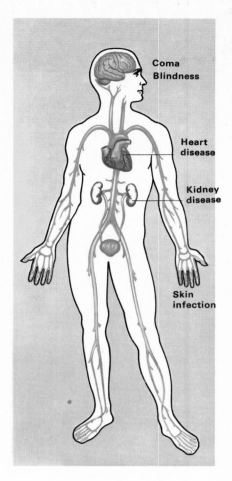

Above: This diagram shows those parts of the body that may be affected in severe diabetes. The most serious is a *coma*, a state of deep unconsciousness.

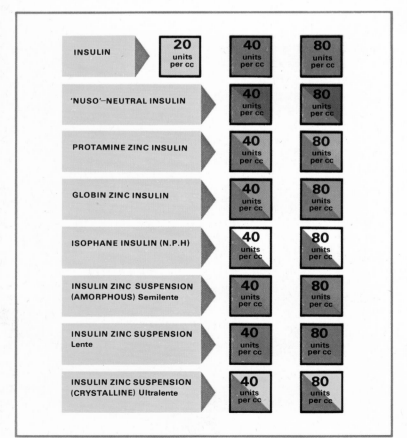

Left: This is a chart to show some of the types and makes of insulin available for treating diabetes. The different colours on the packs are to ensure that the right types and strengths are given to the patient by the chemist following the doctor's prescription.

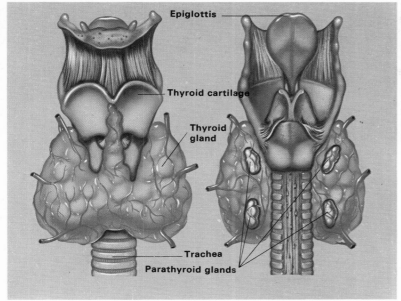

Epiglottis

Thyroid cartilage

Thyroid gland

Trachea

Parathyroid glands

Left: A front view of the thyroid gland (*left*) and a back view (*right*). Without enough iodine in the diet, the gland enlarges to make more, and forms a goitre. The chief thyroid hormone is called thyroxine. It stimulates heat production and metabolism in the body. One of the signs of too much thyroxine from the gland is protruding eyes. This is part of a disease called thyrotoxicosis.

THE THYROID GLAND

The thyroid gland is in the neck. Two lobes of thyroid tissue lie on either side of the voice box connected by a strip of thyroid tissue. Four *parathyroid* glands, each the shape and size of a small pea, lie behind the upper and lower ends of the thyroid.

The chief thyroid hormone is *thyroxine*, which controls the metabolism of the body. *Parathormone* from the parathyroids controls the level of calcium and phosphate in the blood.

Right: Radioactive iodine is used in the diagnosis of thyroid disease. This picture shows the iodine content of the thyroid in colours. Red indicates the highest amount and blue the lowest. In this gland most iodine is in the central part.

HOW A NEW LIFE BEGINS

THE FEMALE SEX GLANDS

The *ovaries* are the female sex glands. Each is the size of a bean and lies in the abdomen on either side of the uterus (or womb), but about eight cm from it. Touching each ovary is the end of a thin tube which leads to the uterus.

From the ovaries come the *ova* (eggs), and the female sex hormones, *oestrogen* and *progesterone*. An interesting fact about the human sex glands is that the male gland, the testis, does not really begin to make sperms until *puberty* (the age at which a boy or girl is physically able to create a new life) but then makes millions every day and can do so for life; whereas a female has up to 400,000 ova at birth, but at puberty has only about 10,000. Of these only one a month develops fully during the whole of the time in her life that she can have babies. This is a total of about 400 ova.

Every month, if a female egg is not fertilized, the lining of the uterus is shed, causing it to go out through the vagina. This is called *menstruation*.

In both males and females, the sex glands are controlled by the pituitary gland.

The sex hormones control the development of the ova (or testes) and of sexual characteristics such as the shape of the body, the development of the breasts, the distribution of hair in the body. In boys these changes are accompanied by the deepening of the voice, referred to as "breaking" of the voice.

Below: A front view of the female reproductive organs as they lie in the abdomen. The cervix is the part of the womb that opens into the birth canal (vagina). The Fallopian tube is the path down which the eggs travel to the womb.

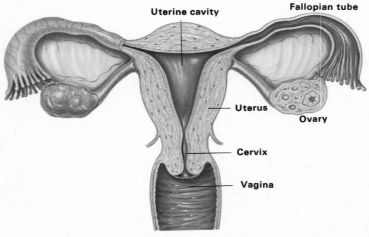

Uterine cavity

Fallopian tube

Uterus

Ovary

Cervix

Vagina

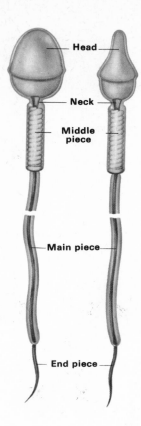

Above: A human sperm magnified many thousands of times. The tail is only 0·05 mm long. It bends from side to side and propels the sperm forward at about 2½ cm a minute. The middle piece is the energy source. The head contains the male chromosomes.

Sex differences also appear in the skeleton. Men have longer arms and legs and broader shoulders than women, but women have broader hips.

THE MALE SEX GLANDS

The *testes* are the male sex glands. They lie in a bag of skin, the *scrotum*, between the top of the legs. They are egg-shaped and four cm long. Looked at through a microscope, they are made up of long, thin, coiled tubes, separated by groups of cells. The tubules produce *spermatozoa* (sperms). The cells produce the male sex hormone *testosterone*.

The *seminal fluid* which the penis pushes into vagina contains many million spermatozoa, but most of the seminal fluid is a nourishing fluid for them. This comes from the *epididymis* (coiled tubes on top of the testis) and the *seminal vesicles* and *prostate gland* near the bladder. A tube connects these structures with the testicles, and in *sexual intercourse* the seminal fluid is expelled through the penis.

During sexual intercourse, the penis becomes stiff because the blood supply to it is greatly increased. The vagina pours out sticky fluid to make an easy entry for the penis. *Ejaculation* is the automatic movement of the semen through the *urethra* at the climax of intercourse in the male.

Right: A side view of the male body cut to show the organs that take part in making a new life. Because of the way the body develops, the sex organs and the organs that excrete waste matter are close together. The tube that runs through the penis, for example, acts as a passage for urine as well as sperms. The *vas deferens* is a tube that takes semen from the testes to the seminal vesicles.

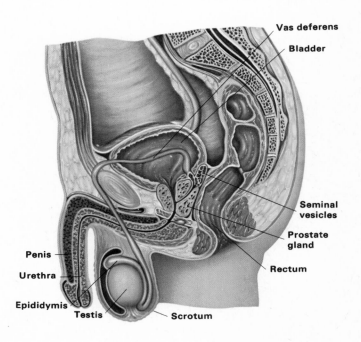

When a man's *penis* is inserted into a woman's *vagina* the sperms emitted in the semen swim up through the uterus (womb) into the tubes joining the uterus to the *ovaries*. If the sperms meet an *ovum* (egg) passing down a tube from the ovary, one of them may join with it (*fertilize it*). The fertilized egg then attaches itself to the inner surface of the uterus and begins the nine-month long growth that turns the egg into an *embryo*, then into a *foetus* (after eight weeks in the uterus) and finally into a new-born baby – a new human life.

SEX DETERMINATION

The moment when the male sperm fertilizes the female egg is the time of *conception*. Whether the new life created then is male or female is already decided. All human cells have 23 pairs of tiny threads called *chromosomes*. One of these pairs of chromosomes is the sex chromosome.

In the female, the sex chromosomes are an identical pair, usually called XX. In the male one of the two sex chromosomes is smaller. It is called Y, and so the pair is XY. When the male sex cell unites with the female sex cell, both have already reduced the number of chromosomes inside them to 23 instead of 23 pairs. So all females eggs will have 22+X chromosomes. But only half the spermatozoa will have 22+X chromosomes. The other half of the spermatozoa will have 22+Y chromosomes.

When one of these 22+Y unites with a 22+X chromosome, a male embryo begins. More boys are born than girls. In Great Britain the ratio of boys to girls is about 105:100.

Chromosomes carry all the information that the newly fertilized egg needs to make a new life. The chromosomes consist of long, thin chains of *genes* – the messengers of heredity. A new life gets half its genes from its mother and half from its father. Genes are made of *DNA*, (deoxyribonucleic acid). The *DNA* can be arranged in thousands of different ways in genes, so that much information can be carried in a minute space. (*DNA* is a molecule, and *molecular biology* is the branch of science that studies it).

TWINS

Dissimilar twins come when two ova are fertilized at the same time. Identical twins are thought to be formed when one fertilized ovum divides into two.

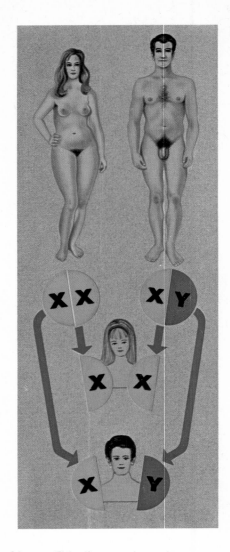

Above: This diagram shows how the chromosomes determine whether a child will be a boy or a girl. The child who inherits the Y chromosome from the father will be a boy.

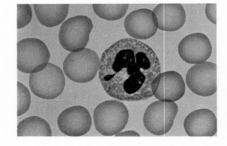

Above: This diagram of a cell nucleus shows the tiny particles of chromatin from which chromosomes are made.

Right: The development of a fertilized egg from a two-celled structure. Each cell divides again and again. At the end of one week after being fertilized, the egg has a hollow centre (*right hand picture*) and is attached to the wall of the womb.

THE DEVELOPING LIFE

About five to seven days after fertilization the egg reaches the wall of the uterus. By this time it has already begun to grow. At the end of the third day after fertilization it consists of 12 cells. By the end of one week it is a larger bunch of cells with a hollow in the middle. Some of these cells become the *placenta*. This is the tissue that nourishes the embryo up to the time of birth when it has almost become a baby.

Other cells begin to form themselves into three layers from which every part of the human body will develop. The outer layer, for instance, will form the skin, the nerves, the inside of nose and mouth. The middle layer forms muscle, blood and bone, the inner layer forms the digestive tract, part of the lungs, and glands such as the thyroid.

At the fourth week after fertilization the embryo is 6 mm. long. The heart begins to beat on the 25th day. Hand, arm and shoulder appear on the 31st day. After the eighth week the embryo is called a *foetus*. It is now possible to see if it is a boy or a girl. At 14 weeks it begins to grow fast. At the 28th week, the foetus weighs an average of nearly $1\frac{1}{2}$ kg. Birth is usually about 38 weeks after conception. An average baby weighs three kg at birth and is 50 cm long.

THE PLACENTA

All this time the foetus has been nourished by the *placenta*, a mass of tissue rich in blood, 18 cm across and $2\frac{1}{2}$ cm thick, on the wall of the uterus. Through it, exchange of oxygen and food between mother and foetus takes place. The *umbilical cord* connects it to the foetus. At the end of pregnancy the uterus contracts to push the newly-formed baby into the world through the vagina. After birth, it then pushes out the placenta.

Below: The foetus lies in a bag in the womb and is connected to its mother by the placenta. Through it, the foetus takes its nourishment and gets rid of waste.

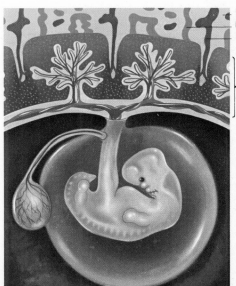

Uterine wall
Maternal artery
Maternal vein

Placental tissue

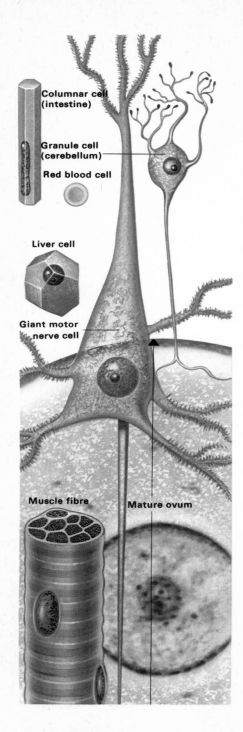

Columnar cell
(intestine)

Granule cell
(cerebellum)

Red blood cell

Liver cell

Giant motor
nerve cell

Muscle fibre

Mature ovum

Above: Some of the many different cells in the human body. An ovum is 0·25 mm across, but an average cell of any other kind is between 0·02 and 0·001 mm across.

CELLS

The human body is made of *cells*. Cells that join other similar cells to do a particular job form a *tissue*. Muscle, for example, is a tissue. The tissues that join other tissues to do a particular job, form an *organ*. The heart, for example, is an organ.

Although cells are of many different shapes and sizes, all cells are very alike in the way they are made. Nearly all cells are too small to be seen without a microscope. Their average width across is between 0·02 and 0·01 mm. When cells are separate and surrounded by fluid, as in the blood, they are often sphere-shaped. But when cells are part of a tissue, the pressure of nearby cells alters the shape. Growth of the cell is another reason for different shapes. Some cells grow into a cylinder shape, or have long shoots from them.

Seen through a microscope, the cell appears to be surrounded by a thin *membrane*. This restricts the passage of materials in and out of the cell, but allows vital substances through.

Each cell is filled with a fluid called the *cytoplasm*, and has a rounded *nucleus* at its centre.

THE CYTOPLASM

The cytoplasm looks grainy, and is a jelly-like fluid containing salts, proteins, fats and carbohydrates. It also contains tiny spheres and tubules containing *enzymes* (substances that aid chemical changes in other substances). Enzymes help in the release of energy from the nourishment brought by the circulation of the cell.

The spheres and tubules are called *mitochondria*. The part of the cell that makes protein from the food brought to the cell by the bloodstream is a network of *RNA (ribonucleic acid)* molecules. Molecules are the smallest part that a substance can be reduced to, without losing its chemical identity.

THE NUCLEUS

The *nucleus* of a cell is rounded. It contains the chromosomes which, as we have seen in discussing inheritance, are made of *DNA*, and so are vital for carrying on life. Cells wear out and need to be replaced. New cells are made through *cell division*.

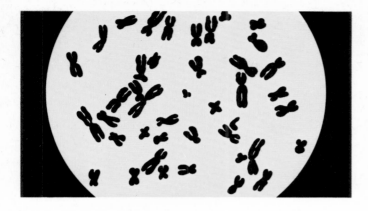

Left: A diagram of human chromosomes, in the nucleus of a cell. They were first discovered in the last century. In 1903 they were found to be connected with heredity. The first correct count of chromosomes was made in 1956. There are 46 in a cell.

CELL DIVISION

The nuclei control cell division. *Mitosis* is the usual way cells divide. Just before a cell divides the chromosomes become doubled. Then, when divided, each new cell has a full 46 chromosomes in it. If the chromosomes had not become like double threads, division would give a cell only 23 chromosomes.

A cell does not take longer than two hours to divide. Not all of them divide at the same pace. Some divide once a day, some once a week, some once a month, or longer.

The study of cells would not have been possible without the invention of the microscope. Now, the electron microscope is used for these investigations. It is one of the most fascinating branches of medicine. It is from the study of cells that scientists one day hope to find the answer to the nature of life itself.

Below: A cell magnified many thousands of times. In the centre is the nucleus. Billions of cells make up the human body.

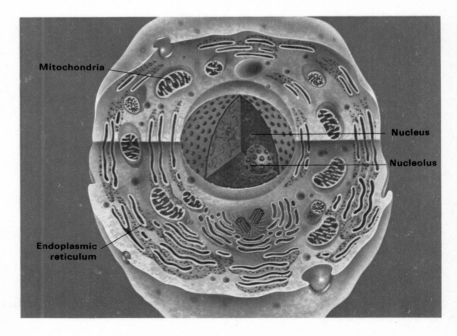

Mitochondria

Nucleus

Nucleolus

Endoplasmic reticulum

INDEX